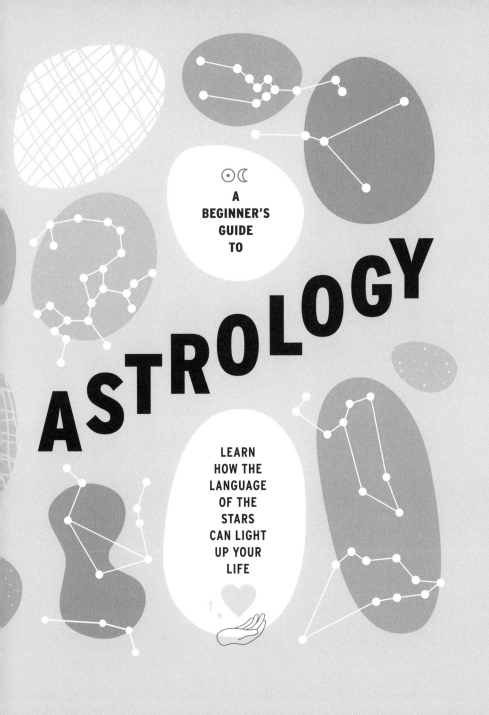

A
BEGINNER'S
GUIDE
TO

ASTROLOGY

LEARN
HOW THE
LANGUAGE
OF THE
STARS
CAN LIGHT
UP YOUR
LIFE

Smith
Street
Books

CONTENTS

INTRODUCTION

Humans have turned to celestial bodies for information and guidance for thousands of years, and probably long before that as well. It is no surprise – during the day the Sun gives us light and life, at night the stars glitter in the sky while the Moon waxes and wanes, glowing ethereally. How could we not be wholly intrigued?

Astrology is the ancient art that gives these skies, and the planets in them, a deeper level of meaning that goes beyond what science, mathematics and the exploration of our solar system can tell us. It is the mythical language of the stars. It is the understanding that we are one small part of an interconnected existence, affected and influenced by the energies of the planets and their movements through the sky. It is an easily accessible way to add a little magic to our everyday lives.

Although the last few decades have seen mainstream astrology reduced to a single horoscopic element, the practice is so much bigger than that, and can offer so much more. It is full of layers and nuance, enhanced by intuition. This ancient art has thoroughly modern uses – it is a timeless tool for understanding the self. For raising our awareness of who we are, where our strengths lie and what our challenges may be. It provides insight into humanity as a whole, our brief but exceptional time here on Earth, and how we can learn to better love ourselves and one another. The following pages are just the beginning. The story of the stars is forever unfolding, and learning how to read it will help you write your own destiny.

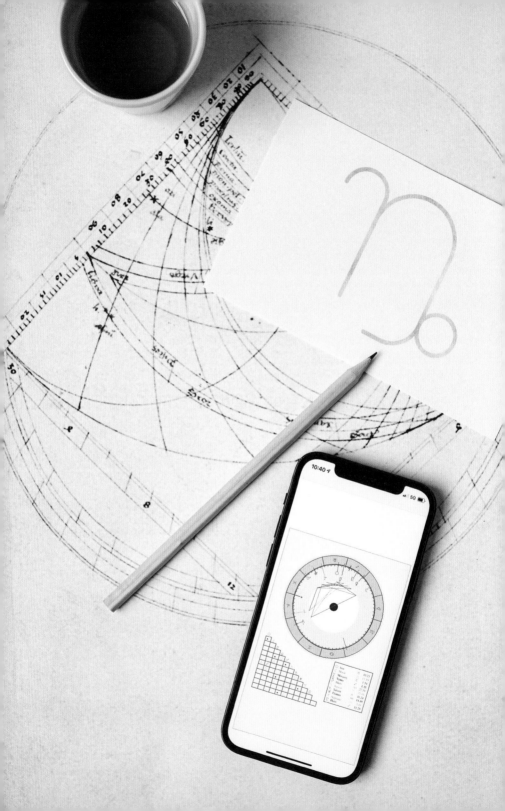

WHAT IS ASTROLOGY?

'The cosmos is within us. We are made of star-stuff. We are a way for the universe to know itself.' – Carl Sagan

Look up at the sky on a clear night, and it just might feel like the gently glowing Moon and brightly twinkling stars are telling a story, one that resonates deep within your soul, vibrating in your very cells. Astrology is the language through which that story is told, a language that humans have been adapting, evolving and utilising since ancient times. It's a language we turn to for understanding and guidance, to feel a part of something beyond our body, to realise our place of interconnectedness with the universe. It's a language full of symbols and archetypes, mythology and mysticism. It's a language that can remind us of the abundance of magic in our everyday lives. But what is astrology?

THE DEFINITION OF ASTROLOGY
At its most fundamental, astrology can be defined as the study of the celestial bodies in our solar system, and how their placement and movement affect us here on Earth. It is the practice of interpreting the planets' patterns, the ways they interact with one another and what that means when it comes to how they influence who we are and how we live.

IS IT REAL?
The foundation of astrology is based on astronomy, the real science that applies physics, maths and chemistry to the study of the celestial bodies outside of the Earth's atmosphere. Astronomy is how we know that the Earth orbits the Sun, that the nearest star is actually close to 6 trillion miles away and that there are more than 200 billion galaxies in our universe – and those are just the ones we can see. But astrology takes these fundamentals of astronomy, of constellations and planets, their placement and movement and steeps it in symbolism, mythology and metaphysics.

There's a reason astrology has captured the hearts and minds of humans for millennia – we see ourselves in it, and we see our essence reflected back. We can regard it as a mind-bogglingly mystical art, while still appreciating its use as a practical tool for self-awareness and a greater understanding of humanity itself. In short, astrology is as real as it feels to you – and as real as you want to make it.

HISTORY OF ASTROLOGY

Astrology is an ancient art with a long and storied journey. It has gone through changes over the years, but its foundation remains intact, just as its inspiration – the glittering, glowing planets we see in the sky – has remained the same.

FROM BABYLONIA TO THE ENLIGHTENMENT

Humans have been looking to nature as a divination tool since the dawn of recorded history, and probably long before that as well. Although the ancient art of astrology has a long and storied past that is difficult to clearly define, its seeds seem to have first been planted by the Babylonians, who, as skilled astronomers, divided the zodiac into 12 parts based on the constellations that the Sun seemed to move in front of throughout the year. Their astronomical and astrological ideas were put into practice by the Egyptians, who believed planetary movements could be predictive. Alexander the Great conquered Egypt around 330BC, thus introducing astrology to the ancient Greeks, who put their spin on it. They laid out the 12 parts of the zodiac into the equal-sized slices of pie of the zodiac wheel that we still reference today (even though, because of the Earth's movement, they no longer match exactly with the constellations they were named for). It is believed that it was around this time that a more horoscopic element was added – emphasis was placed on individual birth charts, and the Greeks applied their ideas behind the four elements (fire, earth, air, water, which you can read more about on page 18) to the zodiac, which became the basis of the Western astrology we think of today. Its popularity spread throughout the Middle East and into Europe, but it wasn't until the 18th century, when a premium was placed on science, that more mystical practices like astrology fell out of favour.

MODERN ASTROLOGY

Astrology rose in popularity once again at the end of the 19th century, along with renewed interest in spiritualism, and continued to gain momentum through the 20th century, when it took on a more psychological tone. Noted Swiss psychiatrist Carl Jung was deeply intrigued by astrology and considered its information to be a 'psychological description of character'. His work and studies of astrology, psychology and the collective unconscious helped shape astrology as we know it now.

ASTROLOGY TODAY

Today, astrology has reached massive mainstream appeal. The proliferation of Sun-sign horoscopes (which were simplified and moulded for use in daily newspapers) over the last century have given way to a much more comprehensive view of astrology. Rather than the simplistic and predictive practice that it had been boiled down to for the last several decades via daily horoscopes, astrology is now considered a powerful framework for better understanding ourselves and our human experience.

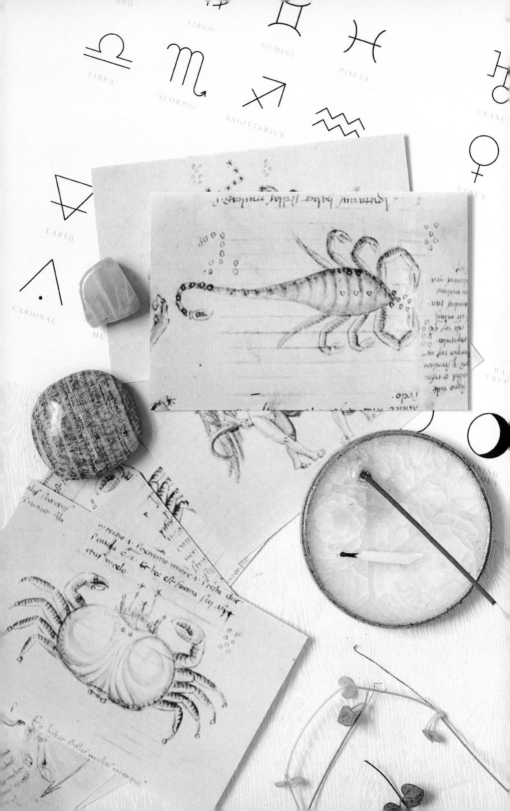

THE BASICS OF ASTROLOGY

Although the following pages delve much deeper into the details, archetypes and characteristics that make up the following concepts, it is helpful to start with an overview of astrology's building blocks.

BIRTH CHART

Your birth chart is a map of our solar system's celestial bodies at the exact time of your birth. It is what reveals your Sun sign (what horoscopes are based on), and so much more. This is how you can get a picture of how you are influenced by the power of the cosmos and its placements when you arrived Earthside (page 137).

PLANETS

There are ten celestial bodies in our solar system that are considered planets by astrology. They include the two luminaries, the Sun and the Moon, as well as the eight other planets that orbit the Sun: Mercury, Venus, Mars, Jupiter, Saturn, Uranus, Neptune and Pluto (which was reclassified as a dwarf planet in 2006, but still holds great importance here). Each planet represents an element of the human experience – for example Mercury rules communication, Jupiter represents growth.

SIGNS

Your birth chart is divided into 12 sections, like pieces of a pie, that represent the zodiac. On your birth chart, each planet will reside in one of the zodiac signs, which are like energetic archetypes, or overarching personalities derived from the essences of human experience, influencing the way that planets express their purpose. If the Sun was in Libra at the time of your birth, then Libra is your Sun sign. But it's not the only sign of importance. Where the Moon was located has a great effect on us too, and the placement of each planet will influence the type of energy exhibited in your life. The sign that was rising on the eastern horizon at your time of birth – your rising sign or ascendant – is important too. Along with your Sun sign and Moon sign, it completes what is known as 'the big three' (page 137).

HOUSES

Knowing the planets and the signs they occupy will give you a basic understanding of your astrological outlook. But there's another major celestial layer to look at: the astrological houses (page 123). Much like your chart is divided into the 12 signs of the zodiac, it is also divided into 12 overlapping houses – each one represents a different area of life, from home to career to belief systems and more. A planet will express its energy through the sign that it falls under and in the house – or the area of life – that it occupies. For instance, if a person has Mercury in the fifth house, which rules creativity, they will likely use the written or spoken word as a means of self-expression.

HOW TO USE THIS BOOK

The following chapters provide an introductory overview of the fun, magical, insightful world of astrology, and how you use this book, much like the practice itself, is entirely up to you. But here are some things to consider as you deepen your understanding of the symbolism of the cosmos, and how you fit into it.

You are probably already familiar with your Sun sign and the energy it expresses. Reading your horoscope might be part of your daily routine, your access to this mystical realm. In which case you may want to turn immediately to the zodiac sign section that your Sun occupies, because it feels familiar and you want to know more. But astrology is so much more than your Sun sign. You may also immediately go online, download your birth chart and be tempted to read only the sections that pertain to you. That's OK too! But astrology also goes far beyond the specifics of a single birth chart.

UNDERSTANDING THE BIG PICTURE

To give yourself the best introduction to astrology, and what it can mean, you will want to start at the beginning of the book and work your way through. This will give you an overview of the practice and help you understand its meaning and symbolism as a whole. It is difficult to grasp what your Sun sign means, if you don't look at your Moon sign and the ways in which it provides some balance. Understanding the shift in meaning from the planets closer to the Sun all the way out towards tiny, distant Pluto, will give you a feel for the full range of characters on the great stage in the sky.

Becoming acquainted with the archetypes of the zodiac, and the energy the signs put forth, will help you understand the nuance of your chart and the different energetic seasons of the year, and of life itself. Becoming acquainted with all the houses will give you a greater understanding of the different areas in your life. But it will also help you to know how to redirect your energy into other areas or in other ways, if what's happening for you now isn't working the way you want it to.

USING ENERGETIC TOOLS

Each zodiac sign chapter includes different crystals and essential oils that both embody the energy of the sign, and help balance it out, along with suggestions for use. Crystals and essential oils are by no means necessary to have a satisfying astrological practice, but they are wonderful tools that can help bring astrology and its energy into the tangible world, and you might find their presence to be incredibly inspiring. That said, the ones suggested are simply that: suggestions. If your Pisces energy resonates more with amethyst than spirit quartz, or if clary sage grounds your Taurus energy more than ylang-ylang, then follow your intuition.

THE SIGNS OF THE ZODIAC

When most people think about astrology, it's the 12 signs of the zodiac that likely come to mind. And for good reason – these 12 signs are the basis of astrology's foundation and play a large role in what the planets can teach us about ourselves.

WHAT IS THE ZODIAC?

Before we delve into the zodiac's influence, it's helpful to understand what the zodiac is. Although we now know that the Sun doesn't move, from our vantage point here on Earth (and to ancient astronomers and astrologers), it certainly looks like it does. And as it crosses the sky (or, more accurately, as Earth orbits the Sun in an elliptical, or oval-shaped, sphere), the Sun passes in front of our celestial sphere's most visible constellations at regular intervals year in and year out.

THE WHEEL OF LIFE

The astrological rendering of this concept is the zodiac wheel, also known as the wheel of life. It is a perfect circle that depicts the Sun's path, divided into 12 equal slices – the signs of the zodiac. Each sign roughly corresponds with one of the zodiac's 12 constellations. The 12 signs represent different human archetypes, or energies, and their cyclical nature can be likened to a journey – beginning with the bold, impulsiveness of Aries when the Sun enters its domain on the spring equinox (in the northern hemisphere), and ending with Pisces, a sign of emotional transcendence and completion.

THE ZODIAC'S INFLUENCE

So how do these fixed sections of the sky, the signs of the zodiac, affect who we are and how we live? The signs do not move, but the planets do, and as the planets move across our sky they travel through the 12 signs of the zodiac. As each planet travels through each sign, the energy of the sign that the planet is 'in' determines how the personality of each planet expresses itself. Mainstream astrology places a huge emphasis on our Sun sign, which is the zodiac sign that the Sun was transiting on the day we were born. As a planet, the Sun represents our core personality (more on that later), which is why we often strongly identify with our designated Sun sign. It plays a huge role in our astrological make-up. But each planet represents a different element of who you are, and they were all in the sky at the moment you came to Earth. The zodiac placement of each planet will affect their influence on you. You may be familiar with the energy of your Sun sign, but getting to know the energy of each sign of the zodiac will give you a much more nuanced and thorough understanding not only of your astrological make-up, but how our daily lives are affected by the planets' transit through the sky.

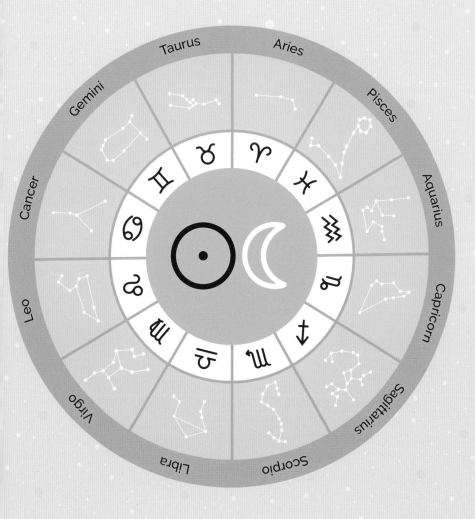

ELEMENTS

Each of the 12 signs of the zodiac falls into one of the four elements – fire, earth, air and water – with three signs ruled by each. Knowing the elements can give you a foundational understanding not only of your Sun sign, but of your chart in general. The more dominant an element is in your chart, the more it will illuminate your nature.

FIRE

Passionate + Driven + Dynamic

Signs ruled by fire: Aries + Leo + Sagittarius

Fire signs are just that: fiery. They tend to be creative, charismatic people with a strong sense of self and a high level of motivation. Fire signs put things into motion, and they often do so with intensity. They tend to command attention (and seek it too!). They are passionate people with deep desires who are not afraid to make those wants known. They are leaders and trailblazers, but can be hotheads too. The flip side of fire signs can be impulsive behaviour, self-centredness and a quick temper. The fire signs' high level of motivation can be infectious, but can also lead to burnout. Intensity is the name of the game, and a challenge for fire signs can be learning how to channel it.

EARTH

Grounded + Practical + Sensual

Signs ruled by earth: Taurus + Virgo + Capricorn

Earth signs have a very down-to-earth nature. They approach the world with an inherent pragmatism and tend to excel in practical matters. They are loyal friends and partners who tend to put down deep roots when it comes to relationships. Earth signs are also attuned to the present, not mired in the past or always thinking of the future. And they are quite in touch with their physical selves as well – they enjoy movement, touch and physical connection. They enjoy the material things life has to offer such as good food, fine wine and material possessions. They are responsible and reliable and find comfort in stability. These traits can also manifest in more challenging ways. Their steadfastness can make earth signs incredibly stubborn and their practical nature can make them averse to taking any sort of risk or stepping outside of their comfort zone.

AIR

Intellectual + Social + Communicative

Signs ruled by air: Gemini + Libra + Aquarius

Air coincides with our mental sphere, and air signs are known for having their heads in the clouds – always thinking. They are quite adept at not only conceptualising their ideas and opinions, but communicating them as well. Air signs tend to be quite social and are able to carry a conversation with just about anyone. They act from a place of rationality rather than emotion, lending a logic to their thoughts and actions. They can move through the world as impartial observers, keenly understanding others' behaviours and motivations. This kind of reserve can have drawbacks as well. Air signs can be known for being somewhat fickle, able to easily move on with a cool and detached demeanour. But they are fun to be around, especially when it comes to sharing new ideas, exploring creative endeavours or simply offering some stimulating conversation.

WATER

Intuitive + Emotional + Spiritual

Signs ruled by air: Cancer + Scorpio + Pisces

Water signs are ruled by emotion. They feel deeply and fluidly – flowing through life and feeling it all, whether the sea is choppy or calm. Water signs tend to be quite highly intuitive, able to sense the emotions of others and empathise with what others are feeling. This means they are often compassionate and able to understand what others are going through. Water signs see everything as a matter of the heart – it always takes precedence over the brain's logic, sometimes to a fault. Because water signs are so open and vulnerable, they can also be especially sensitive, getting easily hurt or overly emotional. Their deep sense of intuition and connection to emotion also means water signs tend to be the most spiritual, able to see our place in the wider universe, and nurture a sense of all that exists beyond our physical world.

MODALITIES

There are three modalities: cardinal, fixed and mutable, which reflect a sign's overarching energy attuned to the Sun's journey through each season. For example, spring (in the northern hemisphere) begins when the Sun enters Aries (cardinal), moves through Taurus (fixed) and exits through Gemini (mutable), before starting the pattern over again with summer.

CARDINAL

Action + Initiative + Achievement

Cardinal signs: Aries + Cancer + Libra + Capricorn

These signs occur at the start of the season, so it is no surprise that they are adept initiators. They know how to make a plan and lay the groundwork for it to be successful. The energy of these signs is all about starting with a bang, such as initiating new ideas.

FIXED

Stability + Steadiness + Sustaining

Fixed signs: Taurus + Leo + Scorpio + Aquarius

These signs represent the middle of the season and as such carry the energy of consistency. They are able to take a plan and put in the work to make it succeed. They are reliable, hardworking, steady and focused, but can also be resistant to change.

MUTABLE

Conclusion + Change + Transformation

Mutable signs: Gemini + Virgo + Sagittarius + Pisces

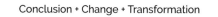

These signs occur at the end of the season and feel quite at home closing a chapter in order to begin another. They carry the energy of change and transformation, adept at letting go and forever going with the flow. They are flexible, allowing new beginnings.

POLARITIES

The broadest categories that the signs are divided into are known as polarities. All of the signs fall into one polarity or the other, and the categories are often designated as masculine and feminine, positive and negative, or active and receptive. They generate the opposite energetic elements that wonderfully complement one another.

MASCULINE/POSITIVE/ACTIVE

Outward-oriented + Assertive

Elements: Fire + Air

Signs: Aries + Gemini + Leo + Libra + Sagittarius + Aquarius

Active signs tend to be outgoing with outward-focused energy. They are comfortably extroverted, tend to forge a more direct path and are driven to take initiative.

FEMININE/NEGATIVE/PASSIVE

Inward-oriented + Passive

Elements: Earth + Water

Signs: Taurus + Cancer + Virgo + Scorpio + Capricorn + Pisces

Receptive signs tend to be more inward-focused – slower, thoughtful and emotional. They are more reactive than active, with a natural inclination towards receptivity and intuition.

♈

ARIES

Confident **+** Adventurous **+** Dynamic

This first sign of the zodiac has all the elements of a leader – confidence, energy, optimism and a go get 'em attitude that loves being in the driver's seat. Aries is full of fire, its corresponding element, and finds itself drawn to new beginnings, indicative of its cardinal energy. New ideas, fresh starts and promising adventures all stoke Aries' need for excitement. They are natural-born leaders, and with their dynamic charisma and an abundance of self-assuredness, others are happy to let them take charge. Aries is appropriately symbolised by the ram – an animal unafraid of butting heads, it evokes the courageous, combative spirit of the sign. Aries knows what it wants and will work enthusiastically to get it. Ruled by the planet Mars, it is in Aries' nature to overcome opponents and triumph over opposition.

Aries is also ruled by the first house of the self, which makes perfect sense for this fiercely independent sign. Aries is self-assured and self-motivated, but it can also be self-involved. Aries likes to get things done, and get them done now – they have little patience for indecision or regret. They act on instinct (which can also mean impulse), and always move forward, never looking back. Their dynamic determinedness can be infectious – Aries energy will make you feel like anything can be done, and that you are the person to do it. Restraint and tact are not their strong suits, but their enthusiasm, optimism and honesty make up for it.

SUN SEASON
21 MARCH–19 APRIL

ELEMENT
FIRE

SYMBOL
RAM

HOUSE
FIRST

RULING PLANET
MARS

OPPOSITE SIGN
LIBRA

MODALITY
CARDINAL

POLARITY
ACTIVE

LOVE, FRIENDS & FAMILY LIFE

For Aries love must mean excitement too – they are as adventurous in their partnerships as they are elsewhere in their lives. They are bold lovers who can make grand romantic gestures, and their fiery nature makes them passionate partners. Fall in love with an Aries and you are ensured a good time! It takes someone truly special and exciting to quell their need for continual newness, but they will be devoted when the right person comes along. Aries likes to lead in the realm of relationships as well, and is happiest with a partner who lets them take charge. Try to rein in their independence and they will be quick to voice their mounting frustration.

Challenges: Aries' restless nature can manifest in relationships, making long-term commitment somewhat difficult. They love the excitement of new partnerships and adventure, so making sure their relationship feeds those desires is imperative. While Aries' self-confidence is often a point of attraction, their self-involvement can leave partners feeling unseen and unheard, especially once the sparkling synergetic newness of the relationship has dulled. Their inclination towards aggression can lead to emotional outbursts, that might not always seem warranted.

Compatible signs: Fellow fire sign Sagittarius has the energy to keep up with Aries, and their mutual love of adventure will keep them seeking it together. Air sign Gemini appreciates the constant mental stimulation and both have a similar need for newness.

Challenging signs: Impulsive Aries will likely find Cancer's caution too frustrating, and these two will find their temperaments at odds. Same with Virgo whose reserved nature and particular way of being will rub against Aries' boldness and need to lead in an unsustainable way.

FRIENDS & FAMILY

Aries is the friend who is up for anything – they have a zest for life that makes everything exciting. You will never be unsure of where you stand with this dynamic sign, they have no problem telling you when they feel slighted, and will likely be the one to speak hard truths aloud. They are generous friends who will support your wildest dreams, and will always have advice for how to make them come true.

They take a similar role when it comes to family. They can be fiercely loyal and staunchly supportive. They like to have the attention of those around them, but they also have a quick temper that can be ignited by family dynamics.

CAREER, MONEY & SELF-AWARENESS

Aries' dedicated determinism helps them excel in the workplace. Their need to succeed will propel them faster and further, no matter what field they end up choosing. Aries' natural inclination to take charge makes them extremely suitable for leadership positions. This sign knows how to make moves – trusting their gut to make swift decisions and put plans into motion. Many find themselves drawn to start-ups or indulging their entrepreneurial spirit, excited to launch the next big thing. Whatever work they do, it must ignite their passion. This enthusiastic sign won't last long in a field that doesn't appeal to their interests or sense of adventure. But if it does, the sky's the limit.

MONEY

Aries tend to be good at making money, but they tend to be good at spending it too. Their impulsive nature extends to the financial realm, and they can have trouble saving for a future that feels eons away, when there's something they see and want right now. Their big, bold personalities manifest in material ways, and they can easily overspend, especially when it comes to chasing new and better experiences. Their short-sightedness can also affect their ability to invest – they may take big risks on the hot new stock because they don't have the patience for long-term growth, only to see their assets plummet when that hot new stock becomes yesterday's news. Learning how to save will be their biggest challenge.

CHALLENGES & SELF-AWARENESS

Recklessness: While decisiveness is one of this sign's more appealing attributes, when their energy runs too hot it can shift from decisiveness to recklessness. Coupled with their need for adventure, Aries can end up moving quickly through life without taking the time to truly consider if where they are going is where they want to be.

Self-absorption: Aries is fuelled by confidence and independence, but too much of the first house energy makes Aries all about themselves. Add to that their drive to succeed, and they can forget who they might be stepping on as they make a beeline for their goals. In interpersonal relationships this means needing to be actively aware of the needs of others, and making room for their ideas and desires.

Follow through: The fiery, cardinal energy is what makes Aries tick, but that need to be propelled can result in a lack of follow through. Their excitement about new ideas and adventures on the horizon, can lead them to change direction before it's time, or leave a trail of unfinished projects in their wake.

CRYSTALS

Crystals are a wonderful way to enhance or balance a particular sign's energies. The following crystals are not only great for Aries, but can also be used by anyone looking to bring some Aries (or Aries-balancing) energy into their life.

ARIES BOOSTING: CARNELIAN

Carnelian is motivation in crystal form. It boosts decision-making skills, vibrates with confident energy and offers assuredness to the voice that needs it. It is a stone of passion and identity, boosting one's sense of self, which is the domain of Aries.

How to use: Hold a piece of carnelian in your hands, while thinking or saying positive affirmations, to boost its power.

ARIES BALANCING: AMETHYST

Amethyst's gentle energy is a soothing balm for Aries' fiery nature. It radiates peace and tranquillity, helping to qualm this cardinal sign's impulsiveness. It's a stone that can help bring harmony, something this combative ram will find helpful.

How to use: A bedside spot is the perfect place for this peaceful stone, creating a tranquil personal space.

ESSENTIAL OILS

Harnessing the wisdom of plants through essential oils, is another way we can work with the energy of the zodiac. These can be wonderful for anyone looking to harness or balance their Aries energy.

ARIES BOOSTING: ROSEMARY

This oil embodies all of Aries' best qualities – it boosts energy, increases mental clarity and improves circulation to get your inner fire pumping. Its mind-clearing properties help banish self-doubt.

How to use: Rub a drop of rosemary oil between your palms, place over your face and inhale deeply. Don't use while pregnant, breastfeeding, or if epileptic or prone to seizures.

ARIES BALANCING: PATCHOULI

This sweet, spicy scent appeals to Aries' sensual side, but is a wonderful oil for supporting mindfulness. It also has a calming quality, helping give pause to Aries' hotheadedness.

How to use: Fill a 10 ml (¼ fl oz) glass roller bottle with sweet almond oil and add 8 drops of patchouli oil. Apply to inner wrists to help boost awareness and calm fiery feelings.

♉

TAURUS

Steadfast + Patient + Dependable

Steadfast Taurus may be the most reliable sign of the zodiac. Their combination of fixed Earth energy makes for a grounded presence, a practical nature and a need for security that nearly trumps all else. Unlike Aries' need for adventure, Taurus is averse to spontaneity and change. This sign feels most at home when the environment is familiar and the circumstances predictable. Taurus energy is slow and deliberate, strong and sensible. Just like the bull that represents this sign, Taurus is a gentle being, until provoked. Their seemingly endless patience does have a limit, and that's when this sign's ferocious nature can flare up.

But Taurus is also ruled by Venus, which makes for an interesting combination of qualities. Although new experiences aren't Taurus's cup of tea, they do appreciate the finer things in life – good food, good drink and good sex too. Taurus energy is deeply sensual and physical pleasures play a large role in their lives. Much like Libra, a sign also ruled by Venus, they have an eye for beauty and a well-heeled aesthetic. They are often drawn to culture and the arts. Perhaps most surprising is the existence of Taurus's inner romantic despite their extremely sensible nature, and an unexpected dreaminess that belies their overt practicality. Taurus is in control, working slowly and unwaveringly towards whatever goal they have set. Whether they will achieve it is never in question, but rather when, and it might be a while – their ability to persist is unmatched in the zodiac.

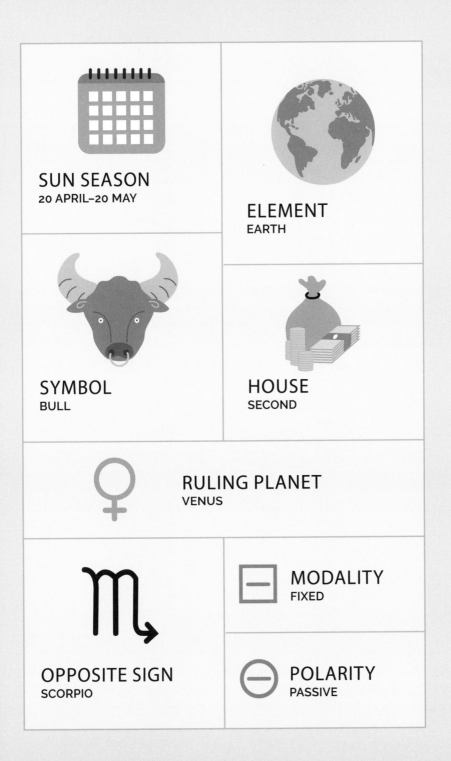

SUN SEASON
20 APRIL–20 MAY

ELEMENT
EARTH

SYMBOL
BULL

HOUSE
SECOND

RULING PLANET
VENUS

MODALITY
FIXED

OPPOSITE SIGN
SCORPIO

POLARITY
PASSIVE

LOVE, FRIENDS & FAMILY LIFE

A Taurus in love is a picture of utter devotion. When they find the right partner, this sign offers a dependable, trustworthy and loving partnership. But this stalwart sign is not looking for a fling. Security is one of Taurus's desires, and that applies to relationships too. They want someone who will be all in, someone they can commit to and build a long and prosperous future with. But they won't make any snap decisions. Taurus is also a sensual being, so the way to their heart is through pampering and pleasure and these simple luxuries go a long way in their eyes.

Challenges: Taurus's dedication can have a downside. This sign's aversion to change can lead to a stubbornness in relationships. Not only causing strife with a partner when Taurus refuses to compromise, but having consequences in the larger picture as well, such as staying in the wrong relationship for longer than they should. Not everyone likes to move as slowly as Taurus, and some might not have the patience for their unhurried way. If Taurus's desire for commitment goes unmatched, it is quite the provocation for their gentle ways, and jealousy can manifest.

Compatible signs: Loyal Cancer is often a good match for commitment-seeking Taurus, and their homebody natures complement one another. Fellow earth sign Virgo is an intellectual match for Taurus, and they appreciate one another's practical, fixed ways.

Challenging signs: Libra is usually much too capricious for this sign; Taurus can't take their flighty, flirty nature. With Scorpio, Taurus meets their stubborn match – these two are very staunch in their ways, which makes long-term love an uphill battle.

FRIENDS & FAMILY

Just as they are devoted partners, they are dedicated friends as well. Their rule by Venus gives them a love of socialising, but rather than flitting around to lots of friendly acquaintances like fellow Venus-ruled Libra, Taurus enjoys a smaller circle of deep connections. Taurus is a friend who will always be there for you, unwavering in their support. Take note though, their sensitive heart may be hurt by something you have done, but their measured nature likely won't let them show it.

Tauruses love a stable home, and this extends to family life as well. Family members are often the trusted ones in Taurus's inner circle (after all they have the long-term, sturdy foundation this sign feels most comfortable with). They also tend to play the family entertainer, hosting holiday meals with impeccable flair.

CAREER, MONEY & SELF-AWARENESS

Career is where Taurus's unique pairing of traits, which combines dreamy creativity with steadfast practicality, can really come into play. This smart, hardworking, congenial sign has the patience and dedication to really dig in and get the job done. Although they are often full of ideas, their love of security makes them shy away from risky endeavours and entrepreneurial leanings. Start-ups are probably not the right place for this sign. But any creative field where they can lean into their down-to-earth nature is – writing, production, event planning or the restaurant industry too. Taurus is a self-motivated worker, so independence suits them just fine. But they are also incredibly easy to get along with, so a team environment works just as well.

MONEY

The financial realm is where Taurus excels. Their dedicated patience, love of luxury and need for security all combine to create a person who is driven to be financially stable. Why spend extravagantly in the present, only to deplete your resources when with patience, you can invest that money, watch it grow and spend extravagantly in the future without compromising your security. Taurus loves the finer things, but they won't spend money they do not have. Their aversion to risk makes them a reliable investor – they may not make millions overnight, but you can bet they will amass a fortune as slow and steady as they please.

CHALLENGES & SELF-AWARENESS

Rigidity: Taurus's fixed nature and grounded sensibilities are what make this one of the most reliable signs in the zodiac. But if they are not careful, they can become too set in their ways, doing something for the sake of familiarity and routine, rather than with intention, and closing themselves off to the wonders of new experiences.

Materialism: Their Venus-fuelled love of all things beautiful, and their utter determination to get what they want, can lead Taurus to seem like a somewhat materialistic sign. Coupled with their ability to gain financial ground, these passions can take over. As long as they are aware of this potential, they should be able to keep their desires in check, without letting them overcome the more meaningful aspects of life.

Uncommunicative: It takes a lot to make Taurus's blood boil, but during that prolonged journey this surprisingly sensitive sign may be bottling up their feelings. Although this sign may be filled with emotions, their reserved nature can lead to a stoic façade, which can dampen their ability for truly intimate connection.

CRYSTALS

Crystals are a wonderful way to enhance or balance a particular sign's energies. The following crystals are not only great for Taurus, but can also be used by anyone looking to bring some Taurus (or Taurus-balancing) energy into their life.

TAURUS BOOSTING: ARAGONITE

This centring stone vibrates with the deeply rooted earth energy of Taurus. It will ground your feet, gently rein in perpetual dreamers as a tether to reality and give your energy a boost. It is also known for cultivating patience.
How to use: Hold a piece of aragonite in your hands while meditating, to help ground your energy as you let your mind flow in peace.

TAURUS BALANCING: CHRYSOCOLLA

The tender open-heartedness of this nurturing stone, can be wonderful for the Taurus who's been keeping their emotions to themselves. Its energy focuses on the heart and throat, boosting compassionate communication. It also helps ease the anxiety of transition.
How to use: Wear a piece of chrysocolla around your neck, to help promote easy, honest and free-flowing communication.

ESSENTIAL OILS

Harnessing the wisdom of plants through essential oils, is another way we can work with the energy of the zodiac. These can be wonderful for anyone looking to harness or balance their Taurus energy.

TAURUS BOOSTING: YLANG-YLANG

Rich, floral and fragrant, ylang-ylang embodies Taurus's sensual side. Its inspiring scent taps into our pleasure centres, appealing to this sign's love of beauty and nurturing its physical nature.
How to use: Add 5 drops of ylang-ylang oil to 1 tablespoon of sweet almond oil and add to a warm bath. This oil may cause drowsiness and may irritate sensitive skin.

TAURUS BALANCING: LEMON

When Taurus feels especially stuck in their ways, lemon can provide the zing they need to open their hearts and minds to change. This citrus scent provides a mental boost.
How to use: Add 1 drop of lemon oil to unscented body lotion and use it to moisturise after a bath. Do a skin patch test first as it may irritate sensitive skin or skin exposed to the Sun.

♊

GEMINI

Clever + Curious + Communicative

Sometimes it seems like this busy sign never stops! Gemini always has a lot going on. This sociable sign loves to make new friends, chat up strangers and share their thoughts and opinions with anyone who will listen. Which comes as no surprise since Gemini is ruled by Mercury, the planet of communication. Gemini's mutable energy also makes this sign very adaptable. This air sign is endlessly curious, constantly seeking out new ideas and experiences, soaking up information like a giant sponge. Mention routine, or any sort of monotony, and flitting, floating Gemini will skip right out the door. Boredom comes fast and furious for this variety-loving sign, and they will go to great lengths to constantly expose themselves to newness. The Gemini mind is quick and their personality playful. They may be the zodiac's most perfect party-goers – skilled conversationalists, enthusiastic people-persons and high-spirited smarties.

This zodiac sign's symbol is the twins, a representation of their penchant for multitasking – a Gemini can get twice as much done in half the time, a testament to their mental acuity and their comfort with a certain level of chaos. Although they are just as likely to finish nothing at all, paving a path of exciting ideas and moving on before they see them through to completion. The twins also symbolise Gemini's capacity for duality, which, when properly channelled, can mean a balance of light and dark, an interest in the realm beyond and that of earthly interests too. This fun-loving sign can sink into deep moodiness as well.

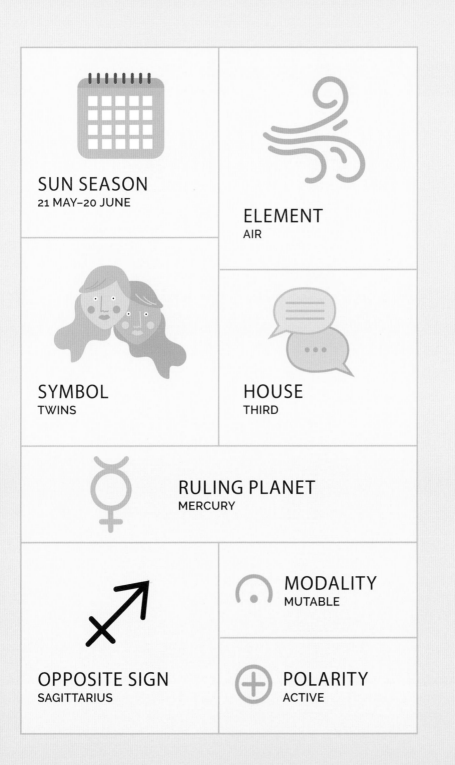

SUN SEASON
21 MAY–20 JUNE

ELEMENT
AIR

SYMBOL
TWINS

HOUSE
THIRD

RULING PLANET
MERCURY

MODALITY
MUTABLE

OPPOSITE SIGN
SAGITTARIUS

POLARITY
ACTIVE

LOVE, FRIENDS & FAMILY LIFE

Geminis are romantic charmers. They are exciting lovers, chatty dates and rapt listeners, as long as you offer up something that piques their interest. But as compelling as Gemini may be, you get the sense that they are never fully present – they have far too much going on to make a habit of commitment. This sign's penchant for variety colours their love life too, and they may dip their toes in one partnership only to have another catch their eye. When they do find their love twin this is when Gemini's giving nature comes out, and their true self is revealed.

Challenges: Because Geminis are always looking for the next new and exciting thing, even when it comes to love interests, they may move on from a potential partner before they have even truly given them a chance. Their tendency for spirited but casual connection can keep them from finding and nurturing a deep and intimate bond. Gemini's charming, flirty, witty nature means there is always someone who will entertain their dalliances – but if they want a lasting partnership, they are going to have to dig deeper, focus their energy and learn to trust and be trusted.

Compatible signs: Libra and Gemini have much in common, including a sparkly sociability and air sign intellect that will keep them engaged for the long haul. Leo's extroversion complements Gemini's enthusiasm, making this fire-and-air pairing an excellent and energetic duo.

Challenging signs: Gemini needs freedom, even within commitment, which makes both Cancer and Taurus difficult matches. Their homebody ways dampen Gemini's need for new experiences. An ill-advised match that makes Taurus possessive and Cancer too sensitive.

FRIENDS & FAMILY

Gemini's social circles are incredibly wide and their calendar is often jam-packed with events. They have all kinds of friends, in all kinds of fields, and this social butterfly spends their time flying from one party/book reading/lecture/art show to the next. They are the fun friend who is always booked, but once you have their attention, they are generous, affectionate and open-minded.

They play a similar role in their family dynamic – adding a wild and adventurous element to the home. But the responsibility of family can sometimes wear on Gemini, who don't want to be tied down by anything, even family obligations to the ones they love. But familial bonds are the ties that bind, so even if Gemini rebels and runs, family is one of the only things they will most certainly return to.

CAREER, MONEY & SELF-AWARENESS

When it comes to career, curiosity reigns. Any field that can keep Gemini's insatiable intellect stoked is one they will excel in. Freelance life often suits Gemini more than a nine-to-five job, since repetition and routine are the fastest ways to dim their spark. Research, writing and media jobs too, can all tap into Gemini's competent communication skills. Anything that leans into their sociability, can also help hold Gemini's typically short-lived attention. With this sign's many varied interests and constant experience-seeking, not to mention mental ability to process and distil it all, most Geminis have their finger on the pulse. It is a skill that lets them thrive in most culture-oriented fields – entertainment, fashion, media and marketing.

MONEY
Being as busy as most Geminis are, doesn't come cheap. A full social calendar can often mean a rather empty bank account – dinners and drinks, car rides and going-out clothes, all of it adds up. Especially for a Gemini too preoccupied with all of the exciting options in front of them, to be bothered to save for a future so far away. Although Geminis tend to have general money luck, they often spend just as much as they make. Their capricious nature can lead to impulse buys and risky investments. Setting aside an automatic deduction for savings, one that Gemini forgets they set up, might be the easiest way for them to build savings, without feeling like they are sacrificing fun.

CHALLENGES & SELF-AWARENESS
Superficiality: Geminis are known for their broad range of interests and their quick-witted minds. But an insatiable curiosity when spread so thin can only retain a rather cursory amount of knowledge. Because of this Geminis might seem rather lightweight – knowing just a little bit about all kinds of things, but not knowing anything truly well or deeply.

Unwillingness to commit: A need for new and constant stimulation, makes it difficult for Gemini to really commit. This can manifest in romantic relationships, of course, but it can also affect what Gemini can get done in everyday life. Finishing projects, seeing through jobs – all of these things can prove challenging for Gemini.

Inability to focus: Busy Gemini may be doing a million things, but how many of those things are they doing well. If one is jumping from one conversation to the next, from one party to another, they will be satisfied on the surface by the quick hits of adrenaline and info. To feel satiated Gemini must learn to slow down, breathe deep and be truly present.

CRYSTALS

Crystals are a wonderful way to enhance or balance a particular sign's energies. The following crystals are not only great for Gemini, but can also be used by anyone looking to bring some Gemini (or Gemini-balancing) energy into their life.

GEMINI BOOSTING: YELLOW CALCITE
Yellow calcite is an energetic stone, radiating with positivity and optimism. It offers a fresh start, clearing the way for new ideas. It also embodies this air sign's information-collecting intellect, helping the mind retain and process all it learns.
How to use: Keep a piece of yellow calcite wherever you do work. It will give you the brain-boosting energy of Gemini's constant curiosity.

GEMINI BALANCING: RED JASPER
This deeply grounding stone is an antidote to chaos and gives Gemini the stability they need when their energy is being diverted every which way. It can help ground Gemini's fleeting curiosity by sparking renewed interest.
How to use: Hold a piece of red jasper, close your eyes and take 3 breaths, inhaling for 6 seconds and exhaling for 8, to enhance a sense of stability.

ESSENTIAL OILS

Harnessing the wisdom of plants through essential oils, is another way we can work with the energy of the zodiac. These can be wonderful for anyone looking to harness or balance their Gemini energy.

GEMINI BOOSTING: BERGAMOT
The complex scent of bergamot is both sweet and spicy, floral and citrus, embodying Gemini's multifaceted character and is known for its mood-boosting properties, just like this air sign.
How to use: Fill a 10 ml (¼ fl oz) glass roller bottle with sweet almond oil and add 12 drops of bergamot. Apply to inner wrists for an uplifting scent. Don't use on skin exposed to the Sun.

GEMINI BALANCING: ALLSPICE
The calming, grounding properties of this spicy oil are wonderful at quieting Gemini's ever-buzzing energies. With notes of cinnamon, clove, nutmeg and pepper, allspice can help bring Gemini into the moment.
How to use: Diffuse allspice at home to create a warm, calm, grounding environment. Don't use allspice internally. It may irritate sensitive skin.

CANCER

Nurturing **+** Sensitive **+** Protective

Deeply emotional but highly protective – of themselves and others – Cancer carries the most maternal energy of any sign in the zodiac. This water sign's symbol is the hard-shelled crab, which scuttles to and fro on the shore then retreats to the sea, just at home in the water as it is on land. Cancer does this too, existing in the material realm but also wading in the watery world of emotions. Cancer's protective shell is difficult to penetrate, which is just how they like it. Underneath is a deeply emotional, sensitive and sentimental soul, that does not want to be vulnerable to the more unsavoury ways of the world. Cancer too is ruled by the Moon, the most emotionally focused celestial body in our sky. Just as the Moon moves the tides, Cancer's moods are mercurial and ever-changing, flowing in and out, and over which they seem to have little control. The gentle, kind and nurturing Cancer, can quickly become crabby, seemingly oversensitive and prone to passive-aggression.

Cancer is also ruled by the fourth house of home. They love to create cosy, welcoming, comforting spaces, which they also love to retreat to when the outside world becomes too much for this sensitive sign. Safety and security are of utmost importance and they will protect theirs at all costs, with a pinch of their claw. But their emotional depth and extreme sensitivity also lends itself to great intuition. They have creative and artistic tendencies, paired with a practical nature and their assertive cardinal energy, Cancer has no problem achieving their goals. But just like their side-scuttling symbol, they won't take the most direct path there.

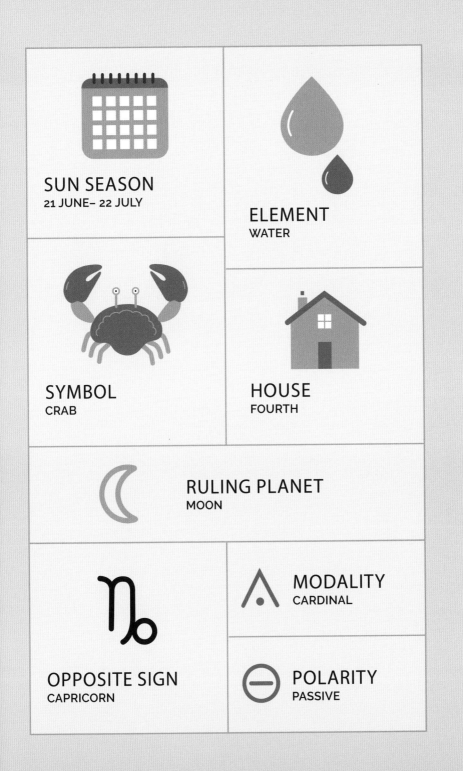

SUN SEASON
21 JUNE– 22 JULY

ELEMENT
WATER

SYMBOL
CRAB

HOUSE
FOURTH

RULING PLANET
MOON

MODALITY
CARDINAL

OPPOSITE SIGN
CAPRICORN

POLARITY
PASSIVE

LOVE, FRIENDS & FAMILY LIFE

Thanks to Cancer's protective shell, getting to know this sensitive sign can be difficult. They may have a reserved façade that can keep potential partners at a distance, but it is just a defence mechanism to protect their inner vulnerabilities and sensitive hearts. Unlike Aries who is direct, and Taurus who is determined, Cancer's advances or invitations will never appear straight on – there will be hints and subtle gestures. In fact, Cancer will never let down their guard until you have built a foundation of trust. But once that bond is built, Cancer is one of the most loyal partners in the zodiac.

Challenges: Cancer's innate nurturing is one of their most beloved traits, but it can also veer into a more controlling nature, especially with a partner who doesn't shower Cancer with the love and reassurance they desire. This Moon-ruled sign's mercurial emotions can also lead to moodiness. When they are feeling oversensitive, a perceived slight may cause them to sulk and initiate the silent treatment. Cancer will rarely take a direct path of communication, which can cause problems with partners if underlying issues are not aired out and addressed.

Compatible signs: Fellow water signs Scorpio and Pisces know and understand Cancer's emotional depth the best. They are adept at navigating changing tides, intuiting what Cancer needs and providing the security that Cancer craves.

Challenging signs: Cancer's appreciation of safety and commitment is rattled by the zodiac's more free-wheeling signs. Gemini's attitude towards love is far too casual for vulnerable Cancer and Aquarius's need to roam clashes with Cancer's homebody tendencies.

FRIENDS & FAMILY

Just as in romantic relationships, one must put in some time to truly get to know Cancer on a platonic level as well. But once you do, this sign is a most devoted friend, offering a dedicated connection of emotional depth. They are quick to help, always supportive, and will welcome you in to their warm and cosy home, happy to host and share their safe space with you. But just as their sensitivity can pose a challenge with partners, they can also retreat from friction with friends, simply re-engaging their protective shell rather than face the issue and work through it together.

Cancer's love of home and security make them especially devoted to their family. This is often where their extreme nurturing manifests, and they tend to play the role of familial caretaker. But their sensitive feelings can be easily hurt, and we all know that harsh words from family can often cut the deepest.

CAREER, MONEY & SELF-AWARENESS

Cancer's caring nature can emerge in a work setting too. They may be seen as the employee who has everyone's best interests in mind, who becomes the office 'therapist', and leaves biscuits or snacks in the communal kitchen. But Cancers are known for their tenacity too – once those pincers grab on to what they want, it is almost impossible to get them to let go. Which is to say they can be very goal-oriented. Cancer makes for a hardworking and dedicated employee, especially if they feel secure in their position. Cancer's elevated emotional attunement can guide them to fields where such sensitivity is an asset – counselling, therapy, human resources, social work. They just need to make sure they take time to disconnect and recharge.

MONEY
Nothing provides security like financial stability, so Cancer is adept with money, allowing them to create the safe home and family life they need. They are good at making money and good at saving it. Their smart business inclination helps them grow the money they do have as well. Their aversion to risk makes them cautious investors, but as watching their wealth grow is important to their mental wellbeing, they spend, save and invest in tried-and-true ways that lets them come out on top. For Cancer, it is not saving they have a problem with, but spending. It is OK to splurge once in a while and enjoy the safe life they have created for themselves.

CHALLENGES & SELF-AWARENESS
Vulnerability: Cancer's shell exists to protect their soft and sensitive soul, but they have to be careful that it does not become too thick. Cancer's nature is to love and be loved, nurture and care, but in order to get to a place where this feels comfortable, they must remove their armour in order to let others in.

Sentimentality: This sign is often steeped in nostalgia and sentimentality, looking to the past and holding on to memories or connections that no longer serve them. Once a Cancer creates a bond, letting go can be the hardest part.

But their journey will be much better served, if they learn to release what should be left in the past.

Insecurity: Feelings of insecurity are one of Cancer's greatest challenges. You may not know from their calm exterior, but internally they may be bubbling with anxiety and self-doubt. At work this can lead to impostor syndrome, believing they are the only one who doesn't know what they are doing. In relationships, both romantic and platonic, it can lead to oversensitivity and neediness, creating an imbalance where none needs to be.

CRYSTALS

Crystals are a wonderful way to enhance or balance a particular sign's energies. The following crystals are not only great for Cancer, but can also be used by anyone looking to bring some Cancer (or Cancer-balancing) energy into their life.

CANCER BOOSTING: ROSE QUARTZ

Just like Cancer is the nurturer of the zodiac, rose quartz is one of the crystal world's most nurturing stones. It vibrates deeply with love and acceptance and evokes a feminine, maternal energy much like Cancer at its best.

How to use: Keep a piece of rose quartz on your nightstand, and let its aura bathe you in true love and acceptance.

CANCER BALANCING: PREHNITE

When Cancer wrestles with issues of insecurity, prehnite can provide the gently powerful self-esteem boost this sign needs. It also helps amplify your ability to speak your mind, and can help you cut ties with elements of the past that no longer serve you.

How to use: Prehnite makes a wonderful pocket stone. Keep it on or near your body when you need some confidence.

ESSENTIAL OILS

Harnessing the wisdom of plants through essential oils, is another way we can work with the energy of the zodiac. These can be wonderful for anyone looking to harness or balance their Cancer energy.

CANCER BOOSTING: CLOVE

This warm essential oil is both sweet and spicy, just like Cancer and their mercurial mood swings. It is also a highly protective oil, warding off germs and viruses with its antiseptic properties.

How to use: Mix a drop of clove with 2 drops of sweet almond oil. Use a finger to dab it on to your skin over your heart. Inhale deeply. Don't use internally or while pregnant or breastfeeding.

CANCER BALANCING: JASMINE

When Cancer's shell has grown too hard, this heady floral scent is a wonderful way to gently open up the heart. It is also known for enhancing feelings of wellbeing.

How to use: Add 3 drops of jasmine oil to 1 tablespoon of sweet almond oil, add to a warm bath and soak in its watery realm. Don't use while pregnant or breastfeeding.

♌

LEO

Warm ✦ Confident ✦ Vibrant

Leo shines brightly, exuding warmth, life and generosity, just like the Sun this sign is ruled by. Leo also likes being the centre of attention, drawing people into their exuberant orbit, just as the planets revolve around the Sun. This sign walks through life with an aura of self-assuredness, a cheerful nature and a penchant for drama. Leos have a deep sense of self and their need for self-expression is quite entrenched. This fire sign is also full of passion, with plenty of energy to get things done, as their fixed nature is accustomed to do. They also tend to be quite playful and cheery, with a magnetism that helps feed their need for the spotlight.

The lion represents this zodiac's sign for good reason. Leo is courageous, never letting the fear of failure stop them in their tracks. They are brave doers, marching forward towards wherever their passion takes them. They do not shy away from a challenge but rather pounce on problems they may face in their path. Lions are also a symbol of royalty, which fits the sometimes self-aggrandising Leo well. This sign believes it is special and important, and is naturally inclined towards positions of authority. This sign is also incredibly big-hearted and brimming with creative energy. Leos live in a perpetual state of abundance. Leo knows they have a lot to give – love, affection, support, ideas – and their deeply generous nature keeps that energy flowing.

SUN SEASON
23 JULY–22 AUGUST

ELEMENT
FIRE

SYMBOL
LION

HOUSE
FIFTH

RULING PLANET
SUN

OPPOSITE SIGN
AQUARIUS

MODALITY
FIXED

POLARITY
ACTIVE

LOVE, FRIENDS & FAMILY LIFE

Leos burn brightest when all the attention is turned towards them. So this sign works best with a partner keen on lavishing them with acknowledgements and praise, who is open to giving their ego the kind of stroking it needs. Under that aura of self-assuredness, Leo is a sensitive soul who needs to be needed. But a Leo partner will give it all right back and more. Leos tend to do and feel everything in a big way, and love is no exception. This sign's vibrant nature is enhanced by partnership – they are honest, faithful, open-hearted and affectionate. They will give a relationship their all, and as their flair for the theatrical implies, will do so with grand romantic gestures and extravagant dates. Attracting the passion of a Leo can be like basking in the warmth and energy of the Sun itself.

Challenges: Leo's grand sense of self can sometimes lead to entitlement. They like to be the king of their kingdom, and sometimes that kingdom can be their relationship. A Leo might take on a somewhat demanding nature, expecting to be served and feeling slighted when they are not. This sign's sense of pride can also get in the way. If they are not given the spotlight they believe they deserve, their unchecked ego can lead to jealousy and resentment.

Compatible signs: Aries and Sagittarius have Leo's fellow fire energy, able to match this sign's larger-than-life character. Both of these signs know how to grab life by the moment, and their sense of joy and passion run on similar paths.

Challenging signs: Taurus's obstinance can clash with Leo's need to rule, while Leo's desire for utter devotion can rub the innate independence of Aquarius the wrong way.

FRIENDS & FAMILY

A Leo friend is a friend indeed. Just as they like to be praised and indulged, they offer the same in spades in return. Turn to a Leo when you need a self-esteem boost, they will be the first to sing your praises, offer support and enthusiastically assure you that you are on the right path, all with sincerity of course. Leo's radiant nature, innate loyalty and love of the spotlight garners them a large and loyal group of friends. And although they won't shy away from a disagreement, they are upfront and honest and do not hold a grudge.

Leos tend to shower their family members the same way. They are overtly affectionate and can play the family cheerleader. They do, however, like to be appreciated for this role, and their pride can be hurt if their efforts are not acknowledged. Leos can be fiercely protective over their loved ones as well.

CAREER, MONEY & SELF-AWARENESS

Leos are passionate, ambitious and hardworking too. A winning combination when it comes to career success. They tend to naturally assume authoritative positions. Friction can arise when this sign is the one who is supposed to be taking direction instead of giving it. And although they love the spotlight, this sign's energy, generosity and enthusiasm tend to make Leo a consummate team player. This sign also thrives in creative fields. Their penchant for theatre makes them natural performers – they tend to be most comfortable when all eyes are on them. But they are likely to excel in any field that lets their creativity reign, allowing them to share their deep sense of self and singular vision with the world (or at the very least, their immediate kingdom).

MONEY

Leo's natural proclivity for succeeding in their field, means they also tend to have a substantial amount of money coming in. But their love of extravagance means it can exit as quickly as it arrived. Saving for the future is not Leo's forte – they live in the moment and want to enjoy it as much as they can, which can mean buying the latest of whatever it is they want, or splurging on dinners, clothes and holidays. Leo's generosity can affect their financial standing as well. It is not unusual for this sign to give great gifts and lend money to any friend or family member who needs it. For Leo, financial stability will come when they manage to save more than they spend.

CHALLENGES & SELF-AWARENESS

Self-centredness: Leo's love for the spotlight can sometimes become too extreme – their need for admiration may become a fixation, eclipsing their better attributes, leading to self-absorption and an inability to truly connect. This sign must remember that an audience isn't everything, and even if they believe they are the star of their show, everyone has a right to their place on stage.

Pride: Leo is very proud, but when their ego becomes outsized it can cause problems if others don't hold them in the same regard. They can become sensitive, losing their joy and even their sense of self. They may suffer indignation that can manifest as jealousy or possessiveness. Leo must remember that it is not the opinions of others that matter, but how they feel about themselves.

Overly dramatic: This sign has a flair for drama. But while a little theatricality can make life more exciting and fun, too much drama can take a turn for the worse, causing Leo to blow things out of proportion or make situations overwrought with emotion.

CRYSTALS

Crystals are a wonderful way to enhance or balance a particular sign's energies. The following crystals are not only great for Leo, but can also be used by anyone looking to bring some Leo (or Leo-balancing) energy into their life.

LEO BOOSTING: SUNSTONE

Leo energy shines bright like the Sun, and sunstone embodies that warmth in crystal form. It radiates with joy and optimism, and is known for increasing generosity as well – one of Leo's most admirable traits. It is a stone that enhances personal power, something Leo is very secure in.
How to use: Keep a piece of sunstone somewhere you can see it through the day. Let it energise your mind and spirit, and raise the vibrations of your home.

LEO BALANCING: HOWLITE

This calming stone can soothe Leo when their fiery elements are feeling out of control. It provides a deep stillness while stimulating creativity. Perhaps most important for Leo, it opens the mind to a higher consciousness, helping to remind this sign that they are not the only player on the stage.
How to use: Hold a piece of howlite in your hands while you meditate, letting it ground your spirit and open your mind.

ESSENTIAL OILS

Harnessing the wisdom of plants through essential oils, is another way we can work with the energy of the zodiac. These can be wonderful for anyone looking to harness or balance their Leo energy.

LEO BOOSTING: GRAPEFRUIT

This bright, citrus scent is like sunshine in a bottle. It has properties that both uplift and energise, much like Leo.
How to use: For a quick hit of happiness, rub a drop of grapefruit oil between your hands, cover your nose and inhale deeply. It may irritate sensitive skin. Don't use on skin exposed to the Sun.

LEO BALANCING: NEROLI

This calming oil eases anxiety while enhancing your mood, allowing Leo to rise up to their greatest traits.
How to use: Diffuse neroli essential oil in the home in the evening to alleviate the stress of the day and create a wonderfully calm environment for sleep. Neroli may cause drowsiness.

♍

VIRGO

Intelligent + Helpful + Pragmatic

Virgo is one of the busiest signs in the zodiac. It is always doing – fixing, solving, cleaning, organising. Virgo is also the most organised sign in the zodiac, it loves to pare down, put things in order, assess the situation – any situation – and make it better. This sign is fixated on fixing. They love when things run smoothly and efficiently and they are on a mission of improvement, not only for themselves, but also for the world at large. And if anyone can make the world a better place, it is Virgo. This earth sign is highly intelligent, and approaches everything from an extremely rational point of view. They love to analyse and have razor-sharp skills in debate, deduction and all kinds of problem-solving. Their world is one of logic – you can always reason with a Virgo.

Sometimes Virgo's analytical viewpoint doesn't leave room for outward emotion, but on the inside this sign can be very sensitive. But they never let feelings get in the way of their pragmatism. They are also driven by a desire to serve. Virgo is one of the most helpful signs in the zodiac. This sign is represented by the virgin, which has little to do with sexuality, and everything to do with the idea of purity. And not only in terms of purity of space – organising and decluttering are among Virgo's favourite pastimes. Virgo's intentions come from the purest of hearts. They are deeply altruistic, wanting to take their stores of facts and data and apply their vast knowledge to helping others.

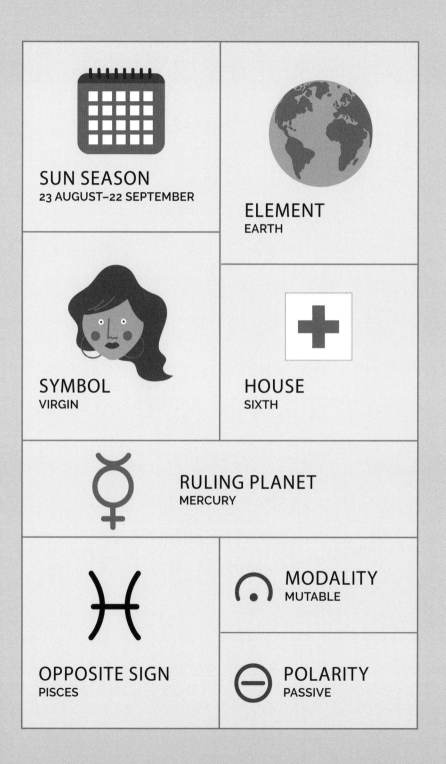

SUN SEASON
23 AUGUST–22 SEPTEMBER

ELEMENT
EARTH

SYMBOL
VIRGIN

HOUSE
SIXTH

RULING PLANET
MERCURY

OPPOSITE SIGN
PISCES

MODALITY
MUTABLE

POLARITY
PASSIVE

LOVE, FRIENDS & FAMILY LIFE

Although this sign is pragmatic in nature, love is what taps into their deep inner emotions. But because Virgo is so self-contained, it may take some time until they allow you in. In the meantime, they may seem somewhat distant or cold, but once they have found a trusted partner, the dam opens up and you will be flooded with affection. Virgo is extremely kind-hearted and trustworthy. Being of service is this sign's love language, so expect them to find ways to make you feel good or make your life better. Their penchant for practicality tends to rule out grand, romantic gestures, but they will do the things that you really need done. Although Virgos appreciate routine, their mutable energy means they can go with the flow, which is helpful in a partnership that requires growth and compromise.

Challenges: Virgo's need to fix can permeate a partnership as well. Although they offer critique and make suggestions for improvement with the best of intentions – they just want to make your life better after all! – it is not always what a partner is open to or interested in hearing. Virgo's downplay of emotions can cause problems too. Not only can it make them difficult to get to truly know, but they may sometimes think with their brain when they should be acting upon what's in their heart.

Compatible signs: Fellow earth signs Taurus and Capricorn can vibe with Virgo's down-to-earth nature. Virgo's rationality complements Taurus's steadfastness while Capricorn's sense of drive and purpose mirrors Virgo's own.

Challenging signs: Leo's exuberant larger-than-lifeness is anathema to Virgo's practical, reserved exterior. Sagittarius's intellect is on par with Virgo, but their free-spiritedness is too much for this orderly sign.

FRIENDS & FAMILY

Unlike prior sign Leo, who loves to be the centre of attention and makes friends with everyone, Virgo tends to be more reserved, preferring intimate interactions to a party situation. Virgo loves an intellectually matched conversation; small talk is not their forte, but they make supportive friends, always ready to lend a helping hand. They tend to fill the role of problem-solver, offering trusted advice unclouded by emotion.

Virgos like to be of use, particularly to their nearest and dearest. They are the family member who's called upon when something is needed. And the same traits that make them the advice giver of their social group can land them in the role of family mediator. Virgo's rational outlook can also help quell family dramas.

CAREER, MONEY & SELF-AWARENESS

Virgo is one of the zodiac's hardest working signs. Their ability to create order where there is none, maximise efficiency and pay attention to even the minutest of details, all while remaining modest and down to earth, means they excel in many workplace environments. Their pragmatism and problem-solving lends itself to certain fields or occupations, and you will often find Virgos in science, law, engineering and analytics. But their drive to serve can draw them to more humanitarian pursuits, like non-profit work or medical fields. Whatever Virgo does they do it thoroughly and they do it well. They are team players who simply want to do the best job possible, whether or not they receive the accolades.

MONEY

Virgo's need for a sense of order usually comes into play in their finances as well. They often have a clear understanding of just how much money they have, how much they need and where it goes – they have a budget and they follow it to a 'T'. Their practical nature tends to make them extremely good savers – problem-solving Virgo is always planning for the future. It also keeps them from extravagant spending, but sometimes that can be the problem. Cautious Virgo will do well to remind themselves that it is OK to behave wildly every once in a while. Go ahead and buy that expensive, impractical item, you probably earned it.

CHALLENGES & SELF-AWARENESS

Perfectionism: While Virgo's need for perfection can make them driven and successful, it can also work against them. Wanting everything to be just so can lead to feelings of overwhelm, frustration, anxiety and burnout. Learning to accept anything less than perfection, will be one of Virgo's great life lessons.

Overly critical: Virgo's problem-solving nature and desire to serve others can often come across as wanted and helpful. But Virgo needs to learn the point at which to pull back, or their good intentions will raise the ire of friends, family, partners and co-workers. No one is free from Virgo's critique, most of all themselves. This sign should be mindful of their inner critic as well.

Too pragmatic: An extremely logical world view is a Virgo hallmark, but there is such a thing as being too rational. Looking only at details and data can dampen inspiration and leave little room for the everyday magic of life. Virgo can also get mired in minutiae, obscuring the bigger picture and not allowing them to pull back and see all the circumstances – and the world – has to offer.

CRYSTALS

Crystals are a wonderful way to enhance or balance a particular sign's energies. The following crystals are not only great for Virgo, but can also be used by anyone looking to bring some Virgo (or Virgo-balancing) energy into their life.

VIRGO BOOSTING: APATITE

Apatite embodies a plethora of Virgo traits. It is known as the humanitarian stone, inspiring a desire to be of service. It is also a great energiser, and enhances the intellect as well, helping you to process all the data you have to make a well-informed path forward.
How to use: Keep a piece of apatite on a surface in your living area to infuse your home with energy and an aura of service.

VIRGO BALANCING: SELENITE

Virgo's mind is always going, with a restless intensity that can be hard to quell. Selenite can be the perfect antidote. It has a powerfully peaceful and cleansing energy, calming the mind and body while raising consciousness, something ever-pragmatic Virgo can certainly use.
How to use: Keep a piece of selenite near your bed; it can help you de-stress after a long and busy day.

ESSENTIAL OILS

Harnessing the wisdom of plants through essential oils, is another way we can work with the energy of the zodiac. These can be wonderful for anyone looking to harness or balance their Virgo energy.

VIRGO BOOSTING: LEMONGRASS

Lemongrass has a little earthiness to its citrus-forward scent, which mirrors Virgo's grounded motivation. It is known for helping to energise the mind and boosting mental clarity.
How to use: For a grounding pick-me-up, rub a drop of lemongrass oil with sweet almond oil oil, then dab onto each of your temples and inhale deeply. Don't use while pregnant or breastfeeding.

VIRGO BALANCING: CLARY SAGE

What Virgo needs most is a salve for their stress. Clary sage is herbal and earthy, bringing instant calm and a deeply grounded tranquillity, while still giving your mental clarity a boost.
How to use: Add 20 drops of clary sage oil to 50 ml (1¾ fl oz) of water in a travel-sized spray bottle, for a de-stressing spray. Shake, spray and inhale. Don't use while pregnant or breastfeeding.

♎︎

LIBRA

Balance + Beauty + Harmony

Libras are the diplomats of the zodiac. They are forever on a quest for fairness, as epitomised by the scales that act as their symbol. Their ultimate goal is balance, and they seek it out in everything they do. Libra is ruled by the planet Venus, which governs love, pleasure and art. Librans often have an eye for beauty, revelling in life's finer things. Their elevated aesthetic permeates all aspects of their lives; not only are Librans drawn to arts and culture, they also often excel in creative fields, as adept at putting their own beauty into the world as they are at appreciating what's already out there.

They tend to be incredibly social creatures, charming anyone and everyone with their effervescence – they are also skilled listeners, always knowing how to make whomever they are speaking with feel like the most important person in the room. They are natural anthropologists, curious about what makes people tick, and eager to figure them out, as an understanding of their desires and motivations can help bring about the harmony they seek.

Because this harmony is so important, Libras often avoid conflict at nearly all costs. They are easy to like, and naturally beloved, effortlessly collecting friendships and romances, although often leaving broken hearts in their wake. Although Libras tend to shower others with attention, it is because they crave that adoration in return. And because of their easy-going nature, inclination for stimulating conversation and engaging energy they often get it.

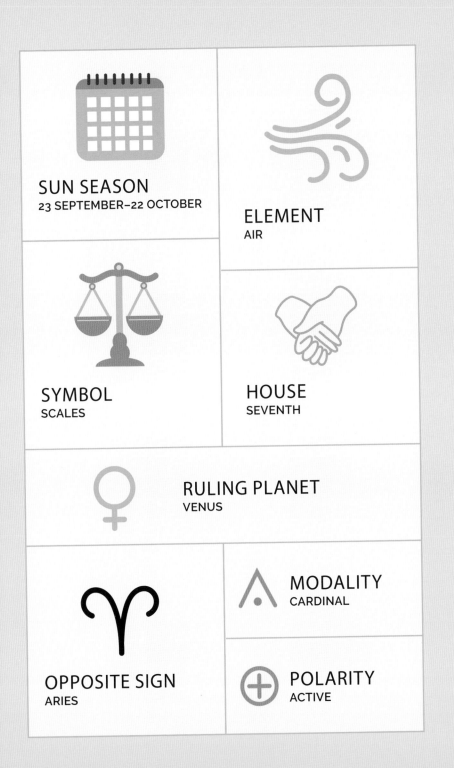

SUN SEASON
23 SEPTEMBER–22 OCTOBER

ELEMENT
AIR

SYMBOL
SCALES

HOUSE
SEVENTH

RULING PLANET
VENUS

MODALITY
CARDINAL

OPPOSITE SIGN
ARIES

POLARITY
ACTIVE

LOVE, FRIENDS & FAMILY LIFE

Libras are in love with love. They love loving and they especially love being loved. Because they are such charismatic people, they rarely want for suitors. They may even be considered the zodiac's ultimate flirts. Libras have a passionate nature and appreciate sensuality and feeling desired. Libra rules the seventh house of partnerships, and as such, Libras often find themselves drawn to relationships. A balanced partnership, someone with whom they can share ideals, and float happily alongside at any and every gathering, helps Libra shine. Just as they like to be adored, they love being in a relationship that is admired by others too. A Libra in love will be in the couple that any single person puts on a pedestal and aspires to be.

Challenges: Because Libras thrive on being loved, romances can burn bright and then fizzle out when the initial stages of excitement have faded. Libras will pull out all the stops when it comes to getting the object of their affection to fall in love, but once they have captured another's heart, they may move on to the next person whose attentions they can dazzle. Although Libra excels at making everything look beautiful, they may have to take a deeper look at relationships, and make sure the inner workings are as appealing as the façade.

Compatible signs: Libras tend to get along with their fellow air signs Gemini and Aquarius. Their equally effortless sociability keeps the harmony for Libra, and their intellectual prowess stimulates Libra's own desire for mental stimulation.

Challenging signs: Capricorns are often too down-to-earth for Libra, not indulging them in their more attention-seeking, capricious ways. Pairing up with a Cancer might be challenging as well, as their home-loving natures are often at odds with Libra's social self.

FRIENDS & FAMILY

Libra's deep desire for harmony really comes through in their platonic and familial relationships. They are the peacemakers, ensuring that everyone in the friend group is happy and getting along. And if there is discord between friends or family members, Libras will naturally fall into the role of mediation, smoothing things over and unruffling feathers, comfortable only when the friction has become water under the bridge.

The natural affability of Libra, along with their penchant for socialising, means that Libra is someone who will know someone everywhere they go. Libras have a wealth of social connections, although they tend to save their most intimate relationships for the few in their inner circle, whether that is family, or chosen family.

CAREER, MONEY & SELF-AWARENESS

Libra's social and affable nature lends itself to people-facing positions. Stick a Libra behind a desk with little human interaction and they will wilt. Customer service, public relations or party and event planning stoke Libra's social inclinations. Libra's creative nature can shine in the realm of career as well. They are often drawn to jobs in the arts – design, fashion, art, writing. Libras like to start new projects and can embrace an entrepreneurial spirit, especially if they have a business partner they feel comfortable with and inspired by, or are able to build a team that rallies round them. Libras quest for diplomacy and fairness lends itself especially well to professions in law, advocacy, human rights and social justice.

MONEY

Libra's sense of balance extends to the financial realm as well. They are smart with their income and can walk the line between spending and saving. They love to be surrounded by beauty, but that doesn't necessarily translate to materialism. A Libra will splurge on that luxurious item that catches their eye, but it will spark joy, which often makes it worth the expense, at least in their mind. Libras can also be generous with their funds, which stems from their desire to be liked – don't be surprised if they pay the bill at dinner, or buy a round of drinks during a night out on the town.

CHALLENGES & SELF-AWARENESS

Indecision: Because Libras are always considering one option against another, and looking at all sides of every situation, they can become paralysed with indecision, or struggle to form an authentic opinion. If they do have a strong opinion, they may shy away from voicing it for fear of confrontation, or upsetting their sense of harmony.

People pleasing: Libra's charming nature can also take a turn towards fervent people pleasing. They may find themselves putting everyone else's needs before their own, and losing their vibrancy, or sense of self in the meantime. Their congenial nature can also at times come across as insincere – although their interest in balance means they can truly agree with all sides of a story; it may seem like they are simply being disingenuous by going along with everything everyone is saying, even, or especially, if those viewpoints are opposing.

Shallowness: The flipside of Libra's love for beauty can lend itself to a certain shallowness. Their role as social butterfly can also lead to over-extension, double-booking events or eventually burning out entirely.

CRYSTALS

Crystals are a wonderful way to enhance or balance a particular sign's energies. The following crystals are not only great for Libras, but can also be used by anyone looking to bring some Libra (or Libra-balancing) energy into their life.

LIBRA BOOSTING: RHODOCHROSITE

Rhodochrosite radiates love and positivity. If Libra's people pleasing stems from low self-esteem, this pink-hued stone can bring an abundance of self-love and acceptance. It is a dynamic stone, vibrating with playfulness.
How to use: Keep a small piece of rhodochrosite in your pocket or handbag to keep its aura of love and acceptance always in your personal space.

LIBRA BALANCING: PYRITE

Pyrite brings Libra's air energy down to earth with its powerfully grounding qualities. It can be beneficial for bringing Libra clarity, when there are too many options being considered. Its glinting gold façade appeals to Libra's need for beauty as well.
How to use: Displaying a piece of pyrite in your work space can keep you focused, while inspiring new ideas.

ESSENTIAL OILS

Harnessing the wisdom of plants through essential oils, is another way we can work with the energy of the zodiac. These can be wonderful for anyone looking to harness or balance their Libra energy.

LIBRA BOOSTING: ROSE

The intoxicating scent of rose is pure romance, almost as if sent by Venus herself. It is a luxurious oil that plays right into Libra's love of pleasure. Rose also has de-stressing qualities.
How to use: Add several drops of rose oil to 1 tablespoon of sweet almond oil and add to a warm bath for a deeply soothing and sensual experience. Don't use while pregnant.

LIBRA BALANCING: EUCALYPTUS

Eucalyptus has an intensely camphorous scent that not only helps centre Libra's air qualities, but also brings focus and clarity to an overwhelmed mind. It is perfect for when Libra is too much in their head.
How to use: Rub a drop of eucalyptus oil in your hands, then place them over your face and inhale deeply to offer immediate rooting to the present. Don't use while pregnant or breastfeeding.

♏

SCORPIO

Passion + Ambition + Transformation

Mystery and intensity are at the forefront of Scorpio. They rise up from a deep well of emotion – it is a water sign after all – which can explode with force or lie seemingly dormant. But despite a calm and collected demeanour, Scorpio's feelings are always relentless underneath. It is all part of the enigma that makes Scorpio one of the most complex signs of the zodiac – one that delves into opposites and extremes, deeply understanding life's greatest shifts and transformations. It is important to note that it is represented by a scorpion – a creature that not only lives but thrives in a desolate desert, far from the water realm this sign is associated with. Just as a scorpion protects itself with a deadly sting, Scorpio might strike when you least expect it.

For Scorpio it comes down to a need for control. They know what they want and will get there by any means, patiently waiting, observing and coolly calculating, until it is time to make their move. Scorpios are incredibly resilient, able to build success out of failure, rebirth after death. There is nothing surface about this sign; they are highly intuitive and can penetrate your façade, quickly able to see through any feigned authenticity. They are not afraid to swim in the deepest waters of their emotions, diving to the darkest depths only to rise up briskly to the surface, even more powerful than before. It may be very hard to crack their shell, but once you have earned a Scorpio's trust, their loyalty, dedication, generosity and kindness knows no bounds.

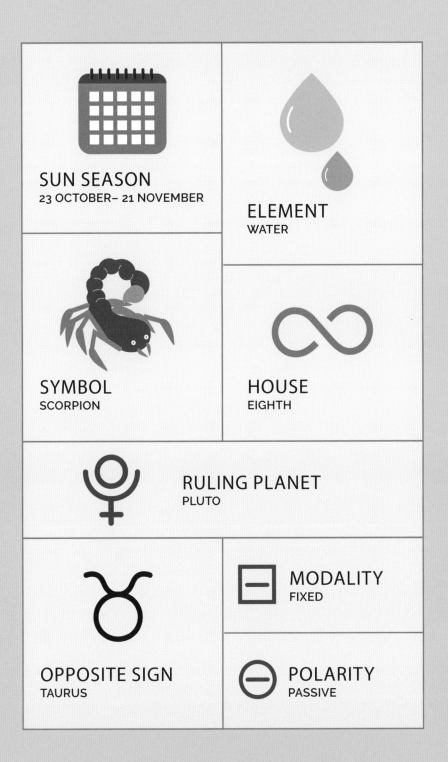

SUN SEASON
23 OCTOBER– 21 NOVEMBER

ELEMENT
WATER

SYMBOL
SCORPION

HOUSE
EIGHTH

RULING PLANET
PLUTO

MODALITY
FIXED

OPPOSITE SIGN
TAURUS

POLARITY
PASSIVE

LOVE, FRIENDS & FAMILY LIFE

Love with Scorpio is an exercise in passion. They love intensely or not at all. It is not always easy to gain entry into Scorpio's realm, but once you do you will be highly rewarded. Because of the deep well of emotion they harbour, they offer a level of intimacy far greater than most signs. Be warned, there is no hiding anything from a Scorpio partner – they can see right through lies and their deep intuition will root out secrets. But offer them a truthful love and they will shower you with affection, stand by you in your darkest hour and explore the deepest depths life and love have to offer.

Challenges: Scorpios demand a great deal of trust, but once that trust is broken there is no going back. Cross a Scorpio once, and you have crossed one forever. Even if that scorn is a perceived one. A Scorpio's need for control can also manifest in ways that are detrimental in a relationship – suspicion and jealousy. Scorpio can be possessive, wanting to be the only one who fulfils a partner's every need. Their emotional intensity can also lead to unpredictability, a relationship roller coaster with wild ups and downs of emotion.

Compatible signs: Scorpios tend to get along with the other water signs, Cancer and Pisces, as they find compatibility in their deeply emotional ways. They can mirror Scorpio's relationship intensity, creating a deeply committed match.

Challenging signs: Freewheeling Aquarius is often too casual when it comes to love to satisfy Scorpio's intense emotional needs. Sparks with Libra may initially fly, but Scorpio's tendency towards jealousy and Libra's naturally flirty nature won't let them last.

FRIENDS & FAMILY

Just as in love, it can be hard to forge a friendship with the ultra-protective Scorpio. They may seem detached or simply too cool, but once real trust has been established, it is a friendship that will travel to the depths of emotion, and offer honest and intimate support when you face life's biggest challenges and transformations – break-ups, births and even deaths. Scorpio's comfort with even the most taboo subjects fosters a platonic intimacy that can only come from knowing each other's deep-seated truths. Scorpios can also be the zodiac's best secret-keepers.

Scorpios also channel their deep devotion into their most committed relationships, which often come from their closest family members. They are extremely loyal and dedicated to taking care of and protecting immediate relatives. It is a bond that is nearly unbreakable. Scorpio is someone you want on your side.

CAREER, MONEY & SELF-AWARENESS

Scorpios are incredibly driven, which means they can excel in almost any work environment. Once they have their sights set on a goal, they will calculate their way to the top, working tirelessly while keeping an unfazed façade, no matter how high the stakes might be. They are great under pressure and can be good in roles that require truth-seeking or emotional depth. Many Scorpios will find themselves drawn to research, medicine or psychology. Regardless of the field though, what Scorpios should always look for is a passion for the work. If they do not find that it sparks their interest and curiosity, they will not find the motivation to succeed. Just as Scorpios can be dedicated partners and friends, they can also be committed to their work.

MONEY
Scorpios love to feel in control and this is true in their financial realm as well. Scorpios can be shrewd when it comes to money – driven to amassing it so that they need to rely only on themselves for financial independence. They know every penny that comes in and every penny that goes out. They also tend to be good at investing, their ability to see beyond what may seem successful on the surface, can lead to highly successful long-term investments. If Scorpios put their calculating nature to good use, it can help them reap big rewards when it comes to their finances.

CHALLENGES & SELF-AWARENESS
Controlling: Scorpio's desire for control can get out of hand if it goes on unchecked. It might take on an obsessive nature, and they might be constantly agitated and aggrieved by all the things that are outside their realm of regulation. A Scorpio must learn to control the things they are able, and learn to loosen their grip on the things that they cannot. This applies to every aspect of their life, from work to home, and family too.

Secretive: The secretive nature of Scorpio can also prevent them from forming friendships and relationships.

It is prudent to want someone to earn your trust, but if you set that bar so high so that it is nearly unattainable, you are simply cheating yourself out of the support and camaraderie that comes with mutually trusting connection.

Emotional: Deep emotions are where Scorpio resides, but this can cause unforeseen challenges. Because it is Scorpio's nature to explore, work through and come out transformed, shunning that curiosity can lead to mood swings and depression. A Scorpio refusing to acknowledge their shadows, is one who will feel perpetually ill at ease.

CRYSTALS

Crystals are a wonderful way to enhance or balance a particular sign's energies. The following crystals are not only great for Scorpios, but can also be used by anyone looking to bring some Scorpio (or Scorpio-balancing) energy into their life.

SCORPIO BOOSTING: MALACHITE

Scorpio is attuned to the process of transformation, and malachite is a stone that helps usher in real change. If you are looking for support when it comes to processing the death of one thing, in order to bring about the birth of another, this green rock will help you do so.

How to use: Place malachite on your nightstand when experiencing big life shifts, as a reminder of the beauty that comes from transformation.

SCORPIO BALANCING: AQUAMARINE

Aquamarine is a stone of calm, perfect for tempering Scorpio's wildly fluctuating emotions. It brings with it a tranquil fluidity, helping you swim through choppy emotional waters. It can also inspire acceptance, something control-oriented Scorpio can benefit from.

How to use: Sit quietly with a piece of aquamarine in your hand, or somewhere nearby, meditating on its cleansing calm.

ESSENTIAL OILS

Harnessing the wisdom of plants through essential oils, is another way we can work with the energy of the zodiac. These can be wonderful for anyone looking to harness or balance their Scorpio energy.

SCORPIO BOOSTING: FRANKINCENSE

Frankincense is an oil as intriguing and enigmatic as Scorpio itself. Its woody, spicy scent has been used for thousands of years in mystical ways, perfect for supporting Scorpio's uncanny intuition.

How to use: Diffuse frankincense at home to create an evocative atmosphere that also provides calming and mood-boosting effects. Don't use while pregnant or breastfeeding.

SCORPIO BALANCING: LAVENDER

When Scorpio's stinger is out, lavender can be one of the best oils for restoring balance and easing the fiery feelings of initiating the strike, whether it was out of fear or anger (or both, as the two often go hand in hand). Its extremely calming properties make it a Scorpio soother.

How to use: Add a drop of lavender oil to your pillow at night to ease any tension from the day. It may cause drowsiness.

↗ SAGITTARIUS

Optimistic + Independent + Adventurous

Sagittarius is the zodiac's wanderer – always looking for life's next great adventure, craving the new and feeling hemmed in by routine. This sign has a deep love of life, and moves through it with a sense of ease and good fortune. Luck befalls you because you tend to believe it will. Sagittarius is the eternal optimist, which is part of what makes them so much fun to be around. They are easy-going rolling stones, forever on the move and enjoying every minute. Sagittarius has a fiery zest for all the world has to offer, and they don't hesitate to chase it down: freedom is their greatest desire. Of course, that coin has another side: any hint of restriction will make Sagittarius rebel.

This sign is also a seeker, not just of experiences that have yet to be had, but of knowledge, truth and wisdom too. Sagittarius is like a sponge, soaking up interests, ideas and new ways of thinking. They view the world through rose-coloured glasses, always working towards their idealistic vision of what life can be. Forever searching for greener grass however, can mean Sagittarius has a hard time appreciating what they have. What you see is what you get with this sign. Unlike the secretive Scorpio, there is no hidden agenda here. Sagittarius is open-hearted and truthful, sometimes to a fault – this sign can embody the term 'brutally honest' without even realising it. Sagittarius is a sign that thrives on expansiveness: of experiences, of the mind, of the world itself.

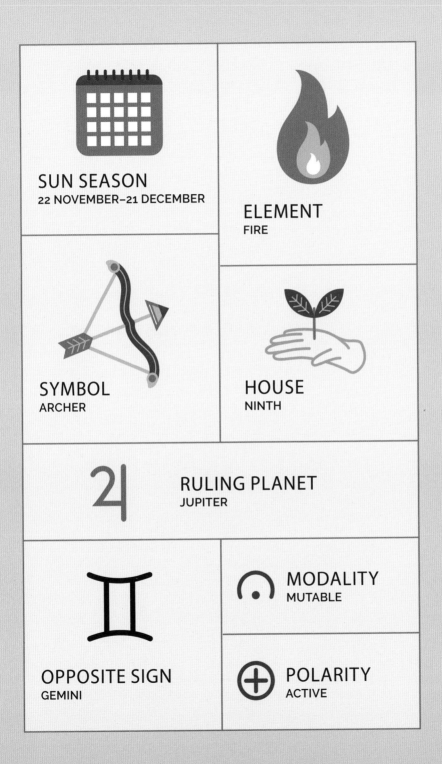

SUN SEASON
22 NOVEMBER–21 DECEMBER

ELEMENT
FIRE

SYMBOL
ARCHER

HOUSE
NINTH

RULING PLANET
JUPITER

MODALITY
MUTABLE

OPPOSITE SIGN
GEMINI

POLARITY
ACTIVE

LOVE, FRIENDS & FAMILY LIFE

Sagittarius's love of adventure translates to relationships too. Each new partner is an exciting experience, an opportunity to learn and explore together. The sign's happy-go-lucky nature makes them a fun partner, continually looking at the positive side of life. For someone who yearns to get outside of their comfort zone, seek out a Sagittarius. They also tend to be spontaneous, which can make for a memorable whirlwind romance. Sagittarius, however, functions best with no strings attached. Their need for freedom tends to trump all, even when it comes to relationships.

Challenges: When it comes to love Sagittarius poses a conundrum – their convivial nature makes it easy to fall head over heels for this sign, but their distaste for routine makes it difficult for them to find success in any long-term relationship. They love the excitement of the new, and although they don't intend to hurt anybody they care about, they can move on quickly when that newness wears off. Sagittarius believes everything will work out in the end, but that doesn't mean doing the work to get there.

Compatible signs: Fellow fire sign Leo is a great match for Sagittarius – both love their freedom and fuel each other's sense of adventure. Same with fire sign Aries; their insatiable curiosities perfectly complement one another.

Challenging signs: Taurus's need for stability and predictability runs antithetical to Sagittarius's innate desire for change. Similarly, Scorpio's need to control is entirely at odds with Sagittarius's most basic need: freedom.

FRIENDS & FAMILY
Although Sagittarius can make a challenging partner for someone looking for long-term love, they make a marvellous friend. They are curious about and supportive of their loved ones' interests, and their generally happy nature makes them endlessly pleasant to be around. Their happiness is contagious, and their free-spirited nature lends itself to fun friendship adventures. Their social circles are wide and eclectic, reflecting their far-reaching interests and curiosities. Sagittarius's open and honest quality tends to build friendships fast, and their ability to bring the party wherever they go, makes them a coveted friend to have.

Sagittarius values their independence, which means they grow up and away from family earlier than most, but this does not affect their deep-seated love and devotion to kin. Even from afar, they cherish the familial bond and always come through when their support is needed.

CAREER, MONEY & SELF-AWARENESS

Sagittarius must be careful when pursuing a career path – their reluctance for any semblance of monotony rules out many typical nine-to-five jobs. This sign thrives doing work that appeals to its need for exploration, whether that means a job that involves literal (and frequent) travel, or whether it is work that allows for expansion of the mind. Many Sagittariuses are drawn to fields of academia and research. They also take well to gig and freelance work – as long as there is always a different project on the horizon, their need for change and variety will not be stifled. The Sagittarius ability to turn anything into an adventure, lends itself to great storytelling – writing, journalism and entertainment are well suited to this sign and its fun outlook.

MONEY

The ease with which Sagittarius seems to move through life, often extends to the financial realm as well. Although they are not particularly good savers – when you live to make every moment even better than the last, you tend to find plenty of things to spend your cash on – they still seem to have just as much money as they need. Just as in life, Sagittarius is comfortable taking big financial risks too, which can often pay off with big rewards. Regardless of their financial situation, Sagittarius will view it with a positive outlook, which always makes them feel like they are in a state of abundance.

CHALLENGES & SELF-AWARENESS

Bluntness: The unfiltered honesty Sagittarius is known for, while often welcomed, can also end up hurting others, causing resentment and fostering misunderstanding. Although it is in their nature to say exactly what they think and feel, it is helpful for Sagittarius to be sensitive to the fact that it might not always be as well received as they expect.

Lack of commitment: The sign's constant need for new experiences and stimulation, can lead to a dearth of commitment in many areas of life. Love for one – Sagittarius must find just the right partner who will not take their need for freedom personally, or they will leave a trail of romantic upset in their wake. While it can lead to exciting travel and interesting ventures, it can also lead to a lack of follow through – abandoned projects, missed deadlines and a shirking of day-to-day responsibilities.

Restlessness: While Sagittarius can shower their friends and partners with love, their restlessness can leave hurt feelings in their wake. Their ability to ditch responsibilities at the drop of a hat, can irk the more loyal signs of the zodiac and leave friends feeling like they are not enough.

CRYSTALS

Crystals are a wonderful way to enhance or balance a particular sign's energies. The following crystals are not only great for Sagittarius, but can also be used by anyone looking to bring some Sagittarius (or Sagittarius-balancing) energy into their life.

SAGITTARIUS BOOSTING: TOPAZ

Things always seem to come easily to Sagittarius, and topaz represents that power of manifestation in crystal form. Just like Sagittarius, it brings joy and also helps facilitate change, which this sign is always seeking. It is a stone of good fortune that vibrates with abundance. **How to use:** Hold a piece of topaz in your hand, then recite a positive affirmation to increase your optimism.

SAGITTARIUS BALANCING: CHAROITE

Charoite is a stone of acceptance, which can help to calm the restlessness inherent in Sagittarius. It helps illuminate the wonder of the present, which this sign can have trouble appreciating. It also promotes empathy, helping Sagittarius understand how their ever-wandering ways might affect those they care about. **How to use:** Keep charoite on your nightstand to help foster a steady sense of acceptance.

ESSENTIAL OILS

Harnessing the wisdom of plants through essential oils, is another way we can work with the energy of the zodiac. These can be wonderful for anyone looking to harness or balance their Sagittarius energy.

SAGITTARIUS BOOSTING: SWEET ORANGE

Sagittarius is the life of the party and sweet orange is the plant world's version. It is a mood boost in a bottle, imparting Sagittarius optimism with every inhale. **How to use:** Add 20 drops of sweet orange oil to 50 ml (1¾ fl oz) water in a travel-sized spray bottle. Shake, spray and inhale. Don't use on skin exposed to the Sun.

SAGITTARIUS BALANCING: GERANIUM

When Sagittarius needs a respite from their restlessness, geranium is an oil that is calming and grounding, helping them to release some of the anxiety that can come with constantly wanting change. **How to use:** Fill a 10 ml (¼ fl oz) glass roller bottle with sweet almond oil and add 10 drops of geranium oil. Apply to inner wrists. Don't use while pregnant.

♑

CAPRICORN

Industrious + Determined + Patient

Slow and steady wins the race for this Saturn-ruled sign, and winning the race is extremely important for the highly ambitious, hardworking Capricorn. When Capricorn sets their sight on a goal, no one and nothing can stand in their way. But rather than blast their way to success, Capricorn takes their time, building a path to the top, one meticulously placed block at a time. This is how they can ensure a sturdy foundation, and it is their endless patience and perseverance that will help them prevail. But just because they are detail-oriented doers, doesn't mean there is no room to dream. Capricorns are creative too, and they simply have the discipline to turn those dreams into reality.

Self-sufficiency is of the utmost importance – a job done well is one Capricorns do themselves. They are decisive, realistic and above all, practical. They are known for taking care of business, which can make it seem like they don't know how to have fun. But underneath that austere exterior is a dry sense of humour just waiting to make you laugh. Capricorn's sea-goat symbol best represents this dichotomy – the industrious goat, securely and steadily scaling the steepest of mountains, but with the tail of a fish, signalling Capricorn's sensitive and emotional undercurrent. It may be hidden, but it is always there. Capricorns always have their eyes on the prize, which can lead them to overlook the wonder of life right in front of them.

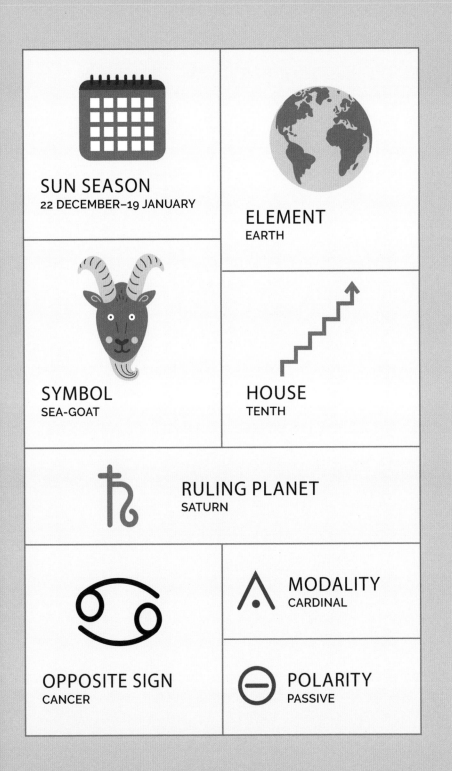

SUN SEASON
22 DECEMBER–19 JANUARY

ELEMENT
EARTH

SYMBOL
SEA-GOAT

HOUSE
TENTH

RULING PLANET
SATURN

OPPOSITE SIGN
CANCER

MODALITY
CARDINAL

POLARITY
PASSIVE

LOVE, FRIENDS & FAMILY LIFE

For the disciplined Capricorn, love is a serious business. They do not play high-risk games with the heart. Capricorn will only put energy in to a relationship if they can see a future where the seeds sown can be harvested. Capricorn has no interest in lighthearted flings or one-night stands. There is no time for something that doesn't get them closer to their goal. But their penchant for hard work can be applied to the personal too; in the right relationship a Capricorn won't give up until all methods of success have been explored. This sign's need for security manifests in the realm of love – Capricorn needs a partner who feels safe, in order for them to connect with.

Challenges: Capricorn's lucky if they have time for love at all – achieving professional and financial success happens to be a time-consuming endeavour. Capricorn's stoic exterior can make them difficult to get to know, and not everyone will have the patience or put in the work to peel away their outer layers of protection. Because of Capricorn's lofty ambitions, they should be especially aware when they are looking for a partner, that they are not only being swayed by their outward success or achievements – they must also like the person not just the pedestal they are on.

Compatible signs: Capricorns tend to pair well with fellow earth signs. Taurus's stability is a relationship bonus, and they are both dedicated partners. Like-minded Virgo meshes well with Capricorn's no-nonsense efficiency and their impressive intellects are a wonderful match.

Challenging signs: Libra's sparkle may catch Capricorn's eye, but this austere sign is too basic for the beauty-loving social butterfly. Sagittarius may appreciate Capricorn's drive, but their need for freedom will be at odds with Capricorn's deep desire for security.

FRIENDS & FAMILY

Capricorns may be hard to get to know, but those who put in the time will be graced with this sign's unwavering loyalty. Rather than a collection of social connections and friendly acquaintances, Capricorns tend to have a handful of very close friends. Just like everything else in their life, Capricorn takes friendship seriously, offering up their well of emotion to those who have earned it, and being steadfast in their platonic support.

Family is also a Capricorn priority. They already know the rewards of this long-term investment – putting energy into familial relationships is a key to success. They are extremely loyal and reliable in this realm, and feel particularly close to family members who know who they truly are.

CAREER, MONEY & SELF-AWARENESS

Capricorns love structure and a clear path to the top. This career-oriented sign can excel in any career that provides a visible ladder to climb. Capricorns often find themselves in leadership positions, by the fact that their diligent work ethic and ambitious efficiency make them desirable leadership material. A career path in which their commitment is rewarded will be the most fulfilling. Because of their goal-oriented nature, and ability to map out a long-term strategy for achievement, Capricorns excel at entrepreneurship. Their perseverance coupled with their forward-thinking planning makes starting a business and building it for continued success something that hits right in their sweet spot.

MONEY

It is no surprise that Capricorns are good with money. Because they strive for a deep sense of security, stable finances are a big part of that and they apply their hardworking patience to building wealth as well. They tend to be conservative with money, and while they may not make high-risk investments, they are putting their money to work for them. Because they are always thinking about the future, Capricorns will never splurge today when they could save for tomorrow. They are great at sticking to budgets and feel most comfortable controlling every detail of their financial situation.

CHALLENGES & SELF-AWARENESS

Rigidity: Because Capricorns are so pragmatic, they sometimes only see in black and white, forgetting that there is a lot of grey in the world. They may think that their way is the only way, or if not the only way, certainly the right one. To be fair, it often is, but this is the work that Capricorn must do – allow space for others to explore their options, even if they can see it will not achieve results.

Too goal-oriented: Speaking of results, Capricorns can be so focused on achieving their goals, they can forget that the journey is just as important, if not more so, than the destination.

Their hardworking nature is at the core of Capricorn's personality, but they need to remember that there is more to life – allowing space for spontaneity may be too much to ask.

Vulnerability: Because their emotional side is buried beneath a seemingly rigid façade, many people might overlook Capricorn's deeply sensitive nature. They might not give them the affection or emotional support they crave, thinking they don't need or want it. And Capricorn may have trouble voicing that desire, as it requires a vulnerability that can be difficult for this sign to concede.

CRYSTALS

Crystals are a wonderful way to enhance or balance a particular sign's energies. The following crystals are not only great for Capricorn, but can also be used by anyone looking to bring some Capricorn (or Capricorn-balancing) energy into their life.

CAPRICORN BOOSTING: BLACK ONYX
This inky black stone has many of the characteristics of Capricorn itself. It is incredibly grounding and stable, helping to channel your energies into achieving your goals. It is a stone of productivity and protection, stamina and strength, while also providing a dose of self-confidence.
How to use: Keep a piece of black onyx in sight in your work place, to help keep you focused on what you want to achieve, and confident in your skills to do so.

CAPRICORN BALANCING: MOONSTONE
Moonstone's ethereal beauty and higher-chakra connection helps balance Capricorn's earthy intensity. It vibrates with feminine energy, helping to soften Capricorn's rigid ways.
How to use: Keep a tumbled moonstone in your pocket or handbag – having its gentle energy close at hand will help remind you to relax into the moment and pave the way for higher thought.

ESSENTIAL OILS

Harnessing the wisdom of plants through essential oils, is another way we can work with the energy of the zodiac. These can be wonderful for anyone looking to harness or balance their Capricorn energy.

CAPRICORN BOOSTING: PEPPERMINT
The cool fresh scent of peppermint helps energise and rejuvenate, boosting mental clarity and productivity too – perfect for the high-achieving needs of Capricorn.
How to use: Rub a drop of peppermint oil between your palms, hold over your nose and inhale deeply whenever you need a momentary refresher. Don't use while pregnant or breastfeeding.

CAPRICORN BALANCING: PALMAROSA
The sweetly subtle floral scent of this oil helps relieve the tension that comes from Capricorn's ambitious workload. It also connects with their emotions, drawing them out from their inner hidden spot.
How to use: Add 5 drops of palmarosa oil to 1 tablespoon of sweet almond oil and add to a warm bath. Don't use while pregnant. It may irritate sensitive skin.

AQUARIUS

Independent + Idealistic + Unconventional

Free-thinking, forward-looking, dream-following Aquarius – this might be the most visionary sign of the zodiac, mainly because it is never content to do things the way they are done. Eccentric, open-minded and wholly unconventional, the only thing predictable about Aquarius is their unpredictability. An air sign, their world is one of grand ideas, each one more exciting than the last. And more often than not, they are plotting, scheming and dreaming of ways to make the world a better place. Aquarius is a humanitarian at heart, taking their interest in the way people tick to a macro level about the way the world works (their symbol, the water bearer, is said to be a healer, and the jar of water the world's collective emotions). But don't expect them to get mired in the details – they are simply the ones with the vision; day-to-day duties and mundane minutiae are not the forte of this freedom-loving sign. Faced with a routine, they will run the other way.

Aquarius is also a study in opposites. Ruled by Uranus, the planet of change, it is also a fixed sign. So while Aquarius will march to the beat of their own drum, doing anything and everything as long as the status quo isn't, they can be quite obstinate in their progressive opinions. And while they have the emotional wellbeing of humanity at heart, they themselves prize intellect over feelings, which is why, despite their overt friendliness and sociability, Aquarius can also seem detached and distant. They are, however, extremely community-oriented, and have a knack for getting along with just about anyone, from any and every walk of life. Hang out with an Aquarius and you might be continually surprised, but you will never be bored. They are never anybody but their truest self.

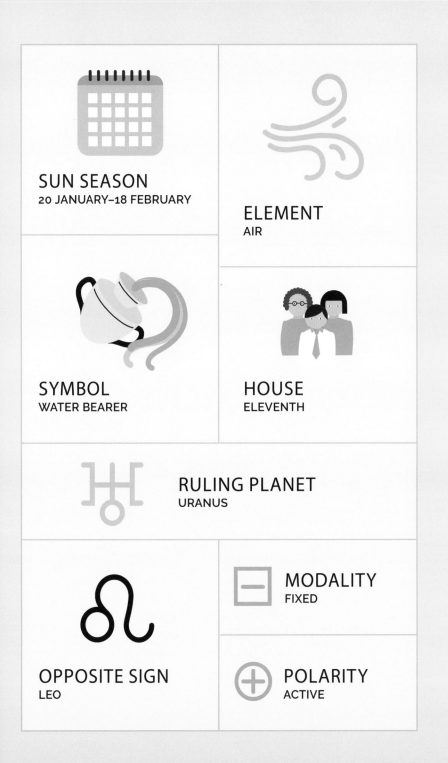

SUN SEASON
20 JANUARY–18 FEBRUARY

ELEMENT
AIR

SYMBOL
WATER BEARER

HOUSE
ELEVENTH

RULING PLANET
URANUS

OPPOSITE SIGN
LEO

MODALITY
FIXED

POLARITY
ACTIVE

LOVE, FRIENDS & FAMILY LIFE

Intellectual stimulation is what puts hearts in Aquarius's eyes. They need someone who can think big like they can. Bonus points if they have a similarly revolutionary style. A partner who wants to help them change the world, is something that might keep this idealist's attention. But throw too many emotions at this air sign too quickly and they will shy away from pursuing a deeper connection. This sign's unconventionality permeates their love life as well – Aquarius doesn't need a conventional partnership, in fact, they are drawn to the opposite. Aquarius is down to try new things to see what works, and that doesn't stop when it comes to love.

Challenges: Aquarius's distaste for tradition and fear of losing their independence, can make them averse to any kind of partnership to begin with. At the first hint of feeling tied down, or made to change their ways, Aquarius will have one foot out the door, and their forward-thinking nature means they won't look back. Their natural inclination to keep feelings at arm's length, can make it difficult to foster the emotional intimacy love thrives on. Even with those they deeply care about, finding that connection might be rather difficult.

Compatible signs: Aquarius is so easy-going, its compatibility runs the zodiac gamut. But, as usual, fellow air signs Gemini and Libra, are a good match in intellect and their similarly social ways. Fire signs Aries and Sagittarius can be good too – neither will try to tie Aquarius down.

Challenging signs: Similarly stubborn Taurus will want to pen Aquarius in, making them run even faster than normal. Scorpio's deep emotions and fiery feelings are often too much for this sign's dispassionate nature.

FRIENDS & FAMILY

While Aquarians might not make the most committed partners, they do however make fabulous friends. Their extremely social, up-for-anything nature makes them someone you want to have around. And the sign's social circles reach far and wide – they have friends in places you would least expect, from every kind of community you can think of. Their loyalty runs deep, even if their emotions don't, although their interest in big-picture ideas may make them overlook the everyday struggles their nearest and dearest are facing.

Aquarius's bucking of the status quo can make them feel like the black sheep of a family, especially if the family dynamic is traditional. But if they are accepted for who they are, relatives get Aquarius at their best – loyal, generous and supportive too.

CAREER, MONEY & SELF-AWARENESS

Just as in relationships, freedom is an important element in an Aquarius's work as well. This sign will always be their eccentric self, so a field in which non-traditionality is an asset is where Aquarius will shine. Their visionary nature leads them to cutting-edge careers – technology or the arts are paths where Aquarius can thrive. The sign's humanitarian streak can manifest in work as well. Aquarius is great at discovering social causes and working to create equity and justice. Many are drawn to non-profit work (as long as they can avoid the nine-to-five office structure) and politics – anywhere they feel like their work is making a difference. Aquarius may carry lofty ideals, but their pragmatism means they can work towards them as well.

MONEY

Although Aquarius is an unconventional rebel at heart, they know money is often the source of freedom, so they are good at saving and can be creative investors too. Just because money is traditional, doesn't mean this sign's way of making, storing or divesting it is. But as good as they are at managing their funds, they are good at spending them too, especially if it satisfies their quest for experience and knowledge. This natural humanitarian also puts money aside for donation, giving to causes that fight for fairness and a better future for all.

CHALLENGES & SELF-AWARENESS

Rebelliousness: Sometimes Aquarius's need to be different becomes rebellion for rebellion's sake, and they need to be diligent about examining their motivations. It is one thing to be contrarian because you believe in the path you are taking; it is another to hold an opinion because it is unpopular. Because their natural inclination is to go against the grain, it is helpful to think critically about why they are doing so.

Stubbornness: This sign will always take the path not travelled, but even if that path is clearly leading to a dead end, their stubbornness will not let them deviate from their choice. Although Aquarius fancies themselves quite open-minded, they often need to apply that regard to assessing their own actions and behaviours as well.

Interpersonal compassion: The humanitarian streak runs deep in Aquarius, but while they focus on helping the collective, they may overlook the needs of the individuals in their lives. Because they have world-changing goals in mind, they may view the daily challenges of their loved ones as unimportant, but to embrace their love of humanity, means finding empathy on a micro level as well.

CRYSTALS

Crystals are a wonderful way to enhance or balance a particular sign's energies. The following crystals are not only great for Aquarius, but can also be used by anyone looking to bring some Aquarius (or Aquarius-balancing) energy into their life. .

AQUARIUS BOOSTING: LABRADORITE

Labradorite embodies some of the most endearing traits of Aquarius – this magic stone contains a flash of iridescence, evoking this sign's independent streak. It helps spark newness into life. It can jumpstart ideas and help bridge the gap between physical and spiritual realms. **How to use:** Place a piece of labradorite on your nightstand to help spark curiosity when you wake, and support your greater visions while you sleep.

AQUARIUS BALANCING: APOPHYLLITE

Apophyllite is a stone of self-awareness, which can help stubborn Aquarius understand the means behind their ways. It also brings an understanding of the interconnectedness of humanity, helping this sign connect with the individual as part of their vision for the greater whole. **How to use:** Meditate while holding a piece of apophyllite in your clasped hands, welcoming its illumination and soaking up its energy of alignment.

ESSENTIAL OILS

Harnessing the wisdom of plants through essential oils, is another way we can work with the energy of the zodiac. These can be wonderful for anyone looking to harness or balance their Aquarius energy.

AQUARIUS BOOSTING: BLACK PEPPER

This spicy scent does its own thing, just like Aquarius. It can give your brain a boost and increase circulation too, enhancing energy. **How to use:** Mix a drop of black pepper oil with a drop of sweet almond oil and dab on to the temples, inhaling deeply. Don't use while pregnant or breastfeeding. It may irritate sensitive skin.

AQUARIUS BALANCING: ROMAN CAMOMILE

The sweetly floral yet fruity scent is calming, giving all that mental Aquarian energy a respite. Roman camomile also supports emotional availability, something this sign can often use. **How to use:** Diffuse at home to create a peaceful space where emotions are welcomed. Don't use while pregnant.

H

PISCES

Sensitive + Intuitive + Compassionate

Otherworldly Pisces is the final sign in the zodiac – the circle's completion, the link to beyond. The last of the water signs, Pisces is ruled by emotion. The symbol of two fish represents Pisces' total submersion – this sign lives in the water, steeped in feelings, swimming in their own and soaking up others' too. While their fellow water signs have elements of protection (think Cancer's hard shell and Scorpio's sting), Pisces is just a giant ball of exposed emotions, swept this way and that, forever floating in the watery realm. Because of this Pisces are highly empathetic, feeling the emotions of those around them, living their days ruled by compassion. The blurred boundaries of their world also make them deeply intuitive, in touch with the inner workings of the human psyche, and able to innately understand what others are going through.

Pisces is a dreamer, living in a world of their own make-up, which holds the utopian characteristics of their ideals, often resistant to what reality actually presents. Pisces is ruled by Neptune, the planet of illusion, and this is often where Pisces prefers to exist. This can also mean Pisces is spiritually gifted, attuned to the energies of this world and others, and open to the mysticism that lies beyond. Pisces' compassionate nature means they are always giving, selfless to a fault. This sign can also be highly susceptible – without a means of protection, they are easily swayed by those around them. Their emotions run deep in both directions, giving them the highest of highs and the lowest of lows.

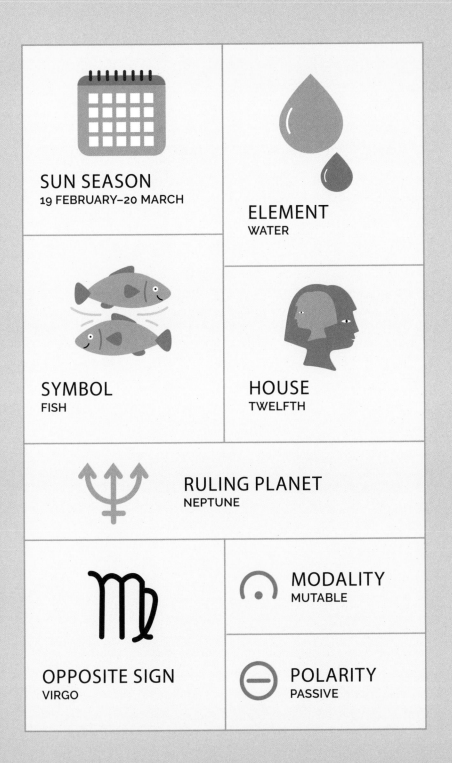

SUN SEASON
19 FEBRUARY–20 MARCH

ELEMENT
WATER

SYMBOL
FISH

HOUSE
TWELFTH

RULING PLANET
NEPTUNE

OPPOSITE SIGN
VIRGO

MODALITY
MUTABLE

POLARITY
PASSIVE

LOVE, FRIENDS & FAMILY LIFE

Pisces otherworldly nature makes them a hopeless romantic, looking for love through rose-coloured glasses. They tend to see the best in people, and are attracted to someone's inner beauty much more than their appearance. More than any other sign in the zodiac, Pisces is looking for a soul connection. They are deeply sensitive and emotional lovers, falling hard and fast and getting easily caught up in the romance of it all. A night with Pisces can be one of pure magic. They are gentle and generous, charming and kind. When a connection is made it is intense. All of the emotions are laid out on the table – this sign values honesty and Pisces doesn't play games.

Challenges: Pisces' bottomless empathy can sometimes backfire, especially when it comes to finding love. They may be drawn to the deeply wounded, forgiving their faults, overlooking bad behaviour and forever trying to nurture them into being a good partner, long after it is probably good for them. This sign's selflessness can pose problems as well. They may find themselves in relationships that don't feel balanced, their mutable nature allowing them to adapt to increasingly inequitable circumstances.

Compatible signs: Fellow water signs Cancer and Scorpio, are two of the only other zodiac signs who can truly understand Pisces' depth of emotion. Cancer's devotion is just what Pisces needs, and Scorpio's otherworldliness lets them connect on a deeper level.

Challenging signs: Pisces might fall for Aquarius's humanitarian streak, but their emotional detachment will be near impossible to overcome. Libra loves Pisces' romantic nature, but will become impatient with the intense emotional support they desire.

FRIENDS & FAMILY

Much like in romantic relationships, Pisces is drawn to their friends' true inner selves – they will see you and love you for who you truly are. They tend to be introverted, but make connections with those in their inner circle. The Pisces friend is generous and available, and they will be there for you in your most emotional times. They are good listeners who are not afraid of feelings, which creates trusted relationships.

The same goes for their family dynamic – Pisces fills the listener role and can often become the emotional support beam of their closest relatives. They are the family member who will be there in your time of need, and they will often intuit when that might be, before you even need to tell them.

CAREER, MONEY & SELF-AWARENESS

The watery Pisces dreamer is an artist at heart. This sign thrives in the creative arts, where they can indulge their ruminations and feeling deeply is an asset. Some Pisces will also lean in to their intuition – they make great tarot readers or energy workers. Their level of emotional intelligence, innate insight and compassion can also lead them to fields like psychology or social work, although they should be careful of getting burnt out by the barrage of other people's feelings. This sign is adaptable, able to work with almost anyone, although their introverted nature lends itself to work with lots of solitary time. Conflict avoidance can be an issue in the workplace, as Pisces may want to keep the peace, even when greater assertion is warranted.

MONEY

Money isn't of great importance to Pisces, they are much more concerned with how the work they do makes them feel. Coupled with their dreamy nature, which tends to make day-to-day financial details like budgeting, bill-paying and saving, money, and everything that relates to it, a challenging realm. If Pisces can view money as a necessary tool that will help them live exactly the life they want, making and managing it becomes something they are much more interested in. Especially since their compassion leads to many loans, paying bills and generous charitable donations, sometimes to the detriment of their own financial security.

CHALLENGES & SELF-AWARENESS

Inequitable relationships: Pisces' lack of emotional boundaries can lead to partnerships and friendships that are not equitable at best, and toxic at worst. But because this sign tends to avoid the messy reality of a situation in favour of their fantasy version, they can stay far too long in these relationships, losing themselves in the process.

Selflessness: This sign's selfless nature can also raise issues. Although Pisces' compassion is one of their greatest strengths, it can also lead to compromising circumstances. A sensitive Pisces in the wrong kind of situation could be easily taken advantage of. Learning to create boundaries and value one's self is at the heart of the Pisces struggle.

Sensitivity: Finding a supportive outlet for Pisces' deep feelings is important or they will not be fulfilled. Whether it is channelling their sensitivity in to the arts or being part of a loving relationship. Creating a stable foundation in these ways, can help give Pisces the validation they need and allow them to blossom in their emotional realm, rather than falling prey to a cycle of self-undoing.

CRYSTALS

Crystals are a wonderful way to enhance or balance a particular sign's energies. The following crystals are not only great for Pisces, but can also be used by anyone looking to bring some Pisces (or Pisces-balancing) energy into their life.

PISCES BOOSTING: SPIRIT QUARTZ

Spirit quartz vibrates on a higher level, a conduit to the unseen world that Pisces prefers. The many points of this sparkling stone magnify its powers to enhance higher consciousness, create harmony and increase compassion, Pisces most meaningful attributes.
How to use: Place a piece of spirit quartz on your nightstand to help connect to your spirituality, and create a healthy space for deep emotions.

PISCES BALANCING: SERPENTINE

When Pisces feels like their emotions have run amok, serpentine is the stone that can bring them back into balance. Its deeply protective powers are both physical and emotional, and it also has a gently grounding effect that will bring the Pisces dreamer back down to Earth.
How to use: Keep a piece of serpentine somewhere that it will be nearby during the day, helping you to set boundaries and regain control of your feelings.

ESSENTIAL OILS

Harnessing the wisdom of plants through essential oils, is another way we can work with the energy of the zodiac. These can be wonderful for anyone looking to harness or balance their Pisces energy.

PISCES BOOSTING: MYRRH

Myrrh has long been associated with mysticism, which appeals to the Pisces' intuitive side. Its heady scent can help give Pisces the dreamy support it needs.
How to use: For a third-eye opening spray, add 14 drops of myrrh to 30 ml (1 fl oz) water in a travel-sized spray bottle. Spray around your head. Don't use while pregnant or breastfeeding.

PISCES BALANCING: CEDARWOOD

Earthy and woody, cedarwood is an oil that helps root Pisces while still supporting their mental state. It is a great way to soothe intense emotions.
How to use: Pisces rules the feet, so add 18 drops of cedarwood oil to 50 ml (1¾ fl oz)sweet almond oil, then use the mixture for a soothing foot massage. Don't use while pregnant or breastfeeding.

PLUTO
Rules: Scorpio
Influences: Power & Transformation

NEPTUNE
Rules: Pisces
Influences: Imagination & Intuition

URANUS
Rules: Aquarius
Influences: Change & Rebellion

SATURN
Rules: Capricorn
Influences: Structure & Discipline

JUPITER
Rules: Sagittarius
Influences: Growth & Luck

MARS
Rules: Aries
Influences: Physicality & Initiative

MOON
Rules: Cancer
Influences: Emotion & Intuition

EARTH

VENUS
Rules: Taurus & Libra
Influences: Love & Pleasure

MERCURY
Rules: Gemini & Virgo
Influences: Communication & Learning

SUN
Rules: Leo
Influences: Identity & Purpose

THE PLANETS

Now that we have a better understanding of the zodiac signs' archetypal energy, we can get to know the planets. It is these celestial bodies, and their movement through the signs, that have the greatest bearing on who we are and how we interact with the world. Each planet represents an element of our personality. Together they create the essence of who we are. Many liken the signs and the houses to an astrological stage in which case the planets can be thought of as actors. It is the placement of these planets at the time of our birth, the different signs and houses they reside in and the ways they travel through the skies of our lifetimes that create our unique astrological picture.

THE LUMINARIES
It shouldn't be a surprise that the brightest celestial bodies in our sky, the Sun and the Moon, are known as luminaries. Go ahead and put your astronomer's hat aside – when it comes to astrology, the Sun and the Moon are considered to be 'planets'. It is the Sun and the Moon that play the biggest role in our charts. (For more detailed information on their particular influences, see pages 96–7.)

THE INNER PLANETS
The planets are organised into three categories based on their distance from the Sun. The first of these are the inner planets: Mercury, Venus and Mars. They are also known as the personal planets, because they affect us in the most personal way, and represent our core characteristics. They are also the planets that move most quickly through the signs. (The Sun and the Moon are both considered to be part of the inner planets.)

THE SOCIAL PLANETS
The next planets in the Sun's orbit are Jupiter and Saturn, also known as the social planets. Unlike the inner planets, which represent bold personality characteristics, the social planets represent how we relate to the world.

THE OUTER PLANETS
Beyond the inner planets and social planets, are the outer planets: Uranus, Neptune and Pluto. These planets are furthest from the Sun, and therefore have the slowest orbits. Because of this, they have less influence on us individually (although their placement is still unique in our own chart), and more influence on the collective, helping to define a generation or an era.

⊙

THE SUN

Identity ✦ Purpose ✦ Creativity

Ruling Sign: Leo

Transit Time: 1 month

It should be no surprise that this blazing ball of fire rules over the ego. It burns with masculine – or active – energy, powerful enough to draw everything else into its orbit.

THE PLANET

Although in astrology the Sun is considered a planet, in reality this 'planet' is actually a star – a 4.5-billion-year-old giant inferno of glowing gases that burns intensely at the heart of our solar system. It is also the largest celestial body in our solar system, its gravity causes everything else to rotate around it. At its core it burns hotter than 15 million degrees Celsius (27 million degrees Fahrenheit) and its existence is what gives us life on Earth.

ITS MEANING

In Roman mythology the Sun is personified by the god Sol – his masculine energy inspired an entire cult of worship. It holds a similar place of importance in astrology. The Sun represents our basic personality. It is the strong, compelling celestial body around which all the other planets orbit, and it lays the foundation of who we know ourselves to be.

In our sky it is the Sun that burns brightest, that gives our planet life, that illuminates our every day. And it does the same in astrology too. The Sun is the core of our being. It represents our purpose, our drive, what makes you you. Of all the celestial bodies, it is the Sun that has the greatest influence on who we are as people – what we are meant to do and understand during our time on Earth. This celestial body shines with a burning force, and it in turn impacts how we shine on others and the world. It represents our creativity and our vitality too. It is our journey, lighting the path towards the fulfilment of our greatest self-expression.

THE MOON

Emotion + Intuition + Self-care

Ruling Sign: Cancer

Transit Time: 2–3 days

The Moon is the yin to the Sun's intense yang. It rules the night with its gentle glow, flooding us with feminine – or passive – energy and governing our interior selves.

THE PLANET

One look up after the Sun has gone down and often the Moon is the first thing you will see. That's because it is the biggest and brightest celestial body in our night sky. It is the only one which orbits the Earth, and its pull is what helps make this planet our home. It stabilises the Earth's wobble, helps maintain our climate and is the force behind the ocean's tides, which provide the planet, and humanity, our very rhythm of living. Unlike the Sun, it doesn't shine, but rather reflects the Sun's light. Which is why we have the eight lunar phases, from a new Moon (when the Sun hits its far side rendering it unseeable from Earth) to full Moon and back again.

ITS MEANING

In Roman mythology the Moon is embodied by the goddess Luna, the female presence that provides a complement to Sol, the embodiment of the masculine Sun. In astrology the Moon embodies our most feminine traits. It is a pure feeling, a gentle foundational presence. It is the planet that gives us our inner lives, our emotional depth. It is vulnerable, private and wholly intuitive. If the Sun puts a spotlight on our life's journey – where we are going and how we conduct ourselves to get there – the Moon reflects our natural self, a deep knowing of who we really are.

If the Sun is action, the Moon is instinct. It is no coincidence that this celestial body reflects the Sun's shine. The Moon is the power behind our emotions, controlling the very waters within, from choppy waves to tranquil stillness. It governs our own ability to reflect and helps us tap into our intuition, the knowing of our subconscious. It is the mother figure of the zodiac, bathing us in its maternal energy, governing how we care for ourselves and each other, and how we feel cared for too.

MERCURY

Communication + Learning + Intellect

Ruling Signs: Gemini & Virgo

Transit Time: 3–4 weeks

As the planet closest to the Sun, Mercury is the messenger, and it has a lot to tell us.

THE PLANET

Mercury is the first planet in our solar system, and one of the smallest too. Its placement in the universe means that when it comes to your birth chart, Mercury will always reside either in your Sun sign, or in the sign that precedes it. Being the innermost planet, Mercury orbits the Sun faster than any other, so its influence on our lives is quick and temporary.

ITS MEANING

In ancient mythology Mercury was the wing-footed messenger of the gods – young, beautiful and incredibly swift. This is who the planet is named for and it rules over our ability to communicate. Mercury takes information in – a rational observer soaking up every detail. But Mercury also puts information out. It governs how we perceive the world as well as how we are perceived. As the messenger planet, it determines our intake of information – not only what we see and hear but how we understand it and process it too. Then it comes full circle, ruling the way we express ourselves.

WHAT IT TELLS US

Mercury's position in our birth chart can reveal a great many things, perhaps most importantly your style of communication. Do you speak loudly with purpose or quietly and unsure of yourself? Are you a natural storyteller? Do you prefer a crowd or one-on-one conversation? It can reflect how we learn, and even the subjects we are drawn to. Its placement influences our entire thinking process, from receiving information to assimilating knowledge to expressing our thoughts and opinions.

MERCURY IN THE SIGNS

Aries: Those with Mercury in Aries tend to be clear thinkers and forthright speakers, saying exactly what they mean, often with wit and without mincing words. They have original voices and outspoken personalities. They might be prone to snap judgements, but that's OK, since their instinct is usually right. They may also tend to be impatient and at times argumentative.

Taurus: Mercury in Taurus reflects a slow and steady thinker, someone who approaches learning and decision-making with methodical dedication. They are incredibly pragmatic with a knack for articulate speech although tend to be much less apt at listening. They tend to be a bit intellectually stubborn as well; once they have formed an opinion, they rarely change it.

Gemini: Mercury in Gemini makes one a fast and nimble thinker, interested in a broad range of subjects and prone to mercurial opinions. They tend to be engaging conversationalists, more than happy to share all the fun facts and informational titbits their curious, sponge-like mind has picked up.

Cancer: Mercury in Cancer leads to a sensitive and intuitive communicator. Their emotional input is incredibly attuned and they can respond in a way that truly connects with their audience. Mercury in Cancer is more interested in emotions than facts and tends to process their world view through personal stories and experience.

Leo: Those with Mercury in Leo are confident, charismatic and self-assured speakers. They excel in the art of persuasion, often because they are genuinely enthusiastic and naturally idealistic – two traits that are hard to resist. They may also have a performative flair and a natural inclination towards leadership.

Virgo: Mercury in Virgo creates an extremely analytical thinker. Facts and logic rule this mind, there is likely no place for emotions in the equation. They will look at every side of every situation, then come determinedly to the most rational conclusion. They have a sharp intellect, articulate manner of speaking and a predilection for language too. Just beware of the toll that perfectionism can take!

Libra: Mercury in Libra strives for balance, walking a line that is both practical and creative. They will spend all their time looking at both sides of the story, and still feel challenged to proclaim a steadfast opinion. They tend to be incredibly charming and tactful speakers, guided by their innate desire for diplomacy.

Scorpio: Those with Mercury in Scorpio have the mind of an investigator. They will look under every proverbial rock and uncover each secret in their quest for knowledge and understanding. They are passionate speakers who love a deep and intimate conversation. They also have an emotional intelligence that attunes them to the motivations and desires of others.

Sagittarius: Mercury in Sagittarius leads to a deeply inquisitive mind, always seeking knowledge on an endless journey of curiosity. They tend to be enthusiastic and honest speakers, although their lack of filter can lead to bluntness. They are quick, open-minded thinkers and easy conversationalists who place a premium on freedom of speech.

Capricorn: Mercury in Capricorn creates an extremely practical thinker, driven by process, method and an adeptly calculating nature. Someone with this kind of Capricorn energy, takes things slow, determinedly processing information at their own steady pace, committing every detail to their impressive memory without sacrificing their big-picture view.

Aquarius: The placement of Mercury in Aquarius creates a creative and innovative mind. They observe and learn with an especially keen intellect, tending to stay far removed from emotions. They are on a quest for the truth, and enjoy thinking about broad and large-scale ideas and philosophies, out to push the realm of humanity into the future.

Pisces: Those with Mercury in Pisces are driven by intuition, feeling their way through the input of the world as opposed to any sort of rational, linear thinking. Their dreamy minds are deeply imaginative but paying attention to details is not their strong suit. They are extremely empathetic speakers and are even more adept listeners.

VENUS

Love + Pleasure + Beauty

Ruling Signs: Taurus & Libra

Transit Time: 4–5 weeks

As the only planet named for a female goddess, Venus's traits are steeped in feminine energy.

THE PLANET

Venus is our closest neighbour in the solar system, the second planet from the Sun, and is often described as Earth's twin although the differences are immense. It is also one of the brightest celestial bodies in the sky, second only to the Moon, which shares its deeply feminine vibe. Venus also has phases similar to the Moon, but rather than cycling through them in a month, it takes a full 584 days.

ITS MEANING

Venus is named for the Roman goddess of love and beauty, so it is no surprise that this planet rules over the way we experience love, pleasure, affection and relationships. Its realm is also that of aesthetics and creativity, material goods and finances. There is a lot going on with this pleasurable planet, and all of it is beautiful. Venus governs who, what and how we love – from romance and attraction to pleasure and sensuality to partnership and sociability – and all of it is rooted in what we value. It is an alluring planet of powerful emotions and earthly desires – no wonder humans have been enamoured by it for so many eons.

WHAT IT TELLS US

Venus's position in our birth chart gives us insight into a wide range of nuanced areas, but the primary one is love. Who do you find attractive and who do you attract? What lights up your pleasure centres and keeps the engine of your heart revved? What roles do romance and affection play in your life? But Venus can also tell us how we love outside of romantic relationships – friendships, family and even work partnerships are all ruled. Venus's placement governs our artistic inclinations and how we seek and enjoy all the beauty the world has to offer.

VENUS IN THE SIGNS

Aries: Someone with Venus positioned in Aries, is probably prone to making the first move. Their heart can be impulsive and their desire assertive, which makes for enthusiastic romances that burn fast and bright, but may not always have lasting power. Just be careful to look beyond the thrill of the chase for a truly meaningful partnership.

Taurus: Venus in Taurus brings the bull's steady nature to relationships – as a deeply sensual and romantic person they will certainly fall hard, but it won't happen fast. Their heart is a careful one, feeling out potential partners for as long as it takes before they commit. But once they do, they offer a deep, affectionate and sexually exciting partnership.

Gemini: Those with the placement of Venus in Gemini, are most likely to fall for someone's quick wit and sharp intellect. A mental connection is what sparks the heart, not only in romance, but friendship as well. They will often prefer easy-breezy connections over deeply intimate and emotional ones, and must retain their freedom for a relationship to blossom.

Cancer: Venus in Cancer makes for a tender-hearted friend and lover. Sensitive and romantic, their biggest challenge in love can be an unshakeable sense of insecurity. Any threat to their emotional safety will cause them to retreat and draw the wrath of crabby Cancer's pincers. But when they feel reassured, loyalty, affection and deep emotional bonds flourish.

Leo: Those with Venus positioned in Leo have an easy, magnetic charm about them. They probably have lots of friends and no shortage of suitors – their warm and affectionate nature is hard to resist. That's lucky for them since attention is what they desire – overt devotion might be a relationship requirement, and they tend to see themselves as the ruler of that domain.

Virgo: For those with Venus in Virgo, their love language is loyalty. But they do not give it freely and easily, instead they tend to be cautious when it comes to matters of the heart. But once in a relationship or friendship they tend to be service-oriented, offering support and affection, and whatever else that might be helpful. They just need to keep their nitpicking in check!

Libra: Venus in Libra creates a major lovefest. These are the people most in love with love. They are romantic and idealistic, falling easily for others and often more than one at a time! But thanks to their charming and charismatic ways, others are always falling easily for them as well. Inspiring partnerships of all kinds come naturally for these extremely social people.

Scorpio: Venus in Scorpio makes for truly passionate affairs, and a tendency towards a deeply emotional and intense kind of love that can be all-consuming if they are not careful and aware. A relationship must be built on a solid foundation of trust – any perceived threat can give rise to jealousy and draw Scorpio's protective stinger out.

Sagittarius: For those with Venus's placement in Sagittarius, love is often viewed through the eyes of adventure. The free-spirited energy of the zodiac's archer, means they are often looking for the next target. Early sparks fly and romance runs high, but without a desire to stay put and commit, feelings fade and they are on to the next.

Capricorn: Caution is the name of the game when it comes to love, for those with Venus positioned in Capricorn. Traditional relationships are typically what they are drawn to, and commitment comes naturally for these practical people. Although pragmatism can often overrule emotion, in a relationship they are often loyal, honest and sensual partners.

Aquarius: Venus in Aquarius makes for a truly unconventional lover. Aquarius energy does not like to be boxed in, and they won't be tied down by traditional expectations or relationship parameters. They love their freedom above all else and need a partner who can go with that flow. Their kind and charismatic nature draws many friends and lovers into their orbit, although they may be prone to turn romance into friendship.

Pisces: With Venus in Pisces, love is a realm of tender, nurturing, compassionate connection. The emotions run deep but so too does self-sacrifice. Those with a Pisces placement of Venus can lose themselves in a romantic relationship, or end up giving too much to a partner who doesn't return the favour. They ride the watery emotions and can be pulled under by a love just as fast as they were swept up by it in the first place.

♂

MARS

Physicality **+** Initiative **+** Sexuality

Ruling Sign: Aries

Transit Time: 6–7 weeks

When it comes to the planets, Mars means action. Its masculine characteristics rule our energetic flow.

THE PLANET

Mars may be little (half the size of our planet and the second smallest in our solar system), but this planet is fierce. Thanks to a rocky surface that contains lots of iron oxide, which gets kicked into the atmosphere by its forceful dust storms, the fourth planet from the Sun has a rusty hue, which makes it look bright red when it is visible from Earth. It also has giant volcanoes, appropriate for Mars's explosive nature.

ITS MEANING

The name Mars is derived from the Roman god of war, known for his indomitable spirit on the battlefield, a willingness to charge and seemingly endless reserves of courage and aggression. The realm of this planet falls accordingly in line. Mars rules our most animalistic instincts – physical energy, passion, anger, sex. It dictates our own 'warrior spirit', our sense of competition and how courage manifests in our lives. Our confidence, drive and overall energy all reside under the jurisdiction of Mars. And although Venus may rule romance, pleasure and sensuality, the realm of Mars exists purely in the body, influencing the primal instinct of physical desire and attraction.

WHAT IT TELLS US

The placement of Mars in our birth chart can illuminate our behaviours, and not only in the bedroom. It can tell us about our relationship with willpower, competition, motivation and more. Do you have an unpredictable temper? An impulsive streak that's difficult to control? In what area of your life do your passions lie? When you want something, how hard do you go for it and how quickly do you get it? Mars can also provide insight into how we feel energy in our body and how our physical strength manifests.

MARS IN THE SIGNS

Aries: Mars in Aries is a recipe for assertion. People with this placement know what they want and have no qualms going after it, whether it is a promotion at work or a romantic interest. Their high energy and directness can make them feel like a force of nature, although all this Mars-Arean energy can also make them hotheaded and domineering.

Taurus: Persistence comes naturally to those with Mars positioned in Taurus. They are tenacious and determined, on a slow and steady path to achieve all that they want and desire. They tend to also be deeply sexual beings, deriving great pleasure from physical connection. This celestial bull just has to check its tendency towards stubbornness and watch out for episodes of anger that can slowly fester and then erupt.

Gemini: For those with Mars positioned in Gemini, their energies lie in the mental realm – they are sharp and quick-witted, and prone to mental sparring. If you want to be invited into their bedroom, you will have to titillate their mind first. But Gemini's restless energy can divert their drive, and living so much in their head can put the brakes on actual action.

Cancer: Unlike the assertive energy Mars in Aries elicits, when this fiery planet is placed in Cancer, strength is less overt and the path to success less direct. Their sense of drive tends to be powered by emotion, and they can get what they want by being sensitive to others' needs. Their sexual proclivities are powered by emotion as well and they thrive on their partner's appreciation and engagement.

Leo: Mars in Leo makes for big plans and even bigger action. Those with Mars in this position have a dynamism that helps them lead and typically makes others happy to follow. They exude passion in life and in the bedroom. But they need the full attention, and preferably adoration, of a lover, which they return in kind, with an abundance of playfulness and affection.

Virgo: For those with Mars positioned in Virgo, they have a direct and detailed approach. They are also driven, although it is not overtly apparent. Passion exists, but has its parameters, and they are ruled more by practicality than fiery emotion. Sexuality too runs under the surface and only a trusted partner will see the fullest expression of their desire.

Libra: When Mars is in Libra its actionable energy is hampered by the inclination of the celestial scales to see both sides of an issue. This can lead to paralysed indecisiveness and Libra's aversion to confrontation dampens Mars's aggressive energy. Their desire is stoked by physical beauty, but they rarely do the pursuing instead preferring to be pursued.

Scorpio: Those with a Mars placement in Scorpio have an intensity that leads to unparalleled determination. They have a purpose and work diligently towards it, powered by resourcefulness and their sheer sense of will. They also have a deep sexuality, which can lead to big emotions, like jealousy and possessiveness.

Sagittarius: When Mars is in Sagittarius, the energy can manifest as a bold and daring adventurousness. Although their insatiable need for stimulation can sometimes become reckless. They are enthusiastic doers, whose productivity can be waylaid by all the things they want to do. The same goes for the bedroom – they are passionate and open-minded but may be resistant to commitment.

Capricorn: Mars in Capricorn makes for a force of self-contained, incredibly driven achievement. They forge a path, and work tirelessly to traverse it, overcoming obstacles with sheer stubbornness. Their motivation, however, can be somewhat detached from emotions and this self-control can put parameters on their strong sexuality as well.

Aquarius: The energy of Mars in Aquarius comes through intellectually – non-traditional and forward-thinking ideas that appeal to them mentally will spark the most action. Their battlefield exists on the mental plane and they will fight for what they think is right. Don't try to box them in within the bedroom either – sexual freedom is crucial for Mars-Aquarians.

Pisces: With Mars in Pisces, the energy is emotional. Those with this placement may have a dreamy nature that makes them shy away from confrontation, but a deep sense of empathy will make them fight for those who need it. Sexuality and feelings are one and the same – in the bedroom they are passionate, intimate and seek deep emotional connection.

JUPITER

Growth ✦ Luck ✦ Opportunity

Ruling Sign: Sagittarius

Transit Time: 12–13 months

Moving from inner planets to social ones, Jupiter is a big-picture player, lavishing abundance on us all.

THE PLANET
Jupiter is the largest planet – 300 times the size of Earth – so it is fitting that it represents growth in astrology. It is the fifth planet from the Sun and takes around a year to complete its orbit. It spins on its axis incredibly fast – a day on Jupiter is less than 10 hours long. This speed makes the planet bulge at the equator; if it were wearing a belt, it would have to loosen the buckle, another element that drives home its energy of abundance.

ITS MEANING
Jupiter is named for the Roman god of gods, benevolent and all-powerful. He symbolised wisdom, honour and faith, ruling over the skies as a charitable leader. In astrology Jupiter represents similar ideas. This planet rules our growth – mentally, spiritually and philosophically too. It influences how we are drawn to big-picture ideas, and in what ways we are keen to expand our hearts, minds and higher consciousness. Jupiter is also a planet of good luck and great joy. Accordingly, it offers up boundless optimism and governs our material growth as well, whether or not we come easily into money and possessions and how much prosperity we attract. Celebrations are also Jupiter's realm, along with how outgoing and successful we are.

WHAT IT TELLS US
Jupiter's position in our birth chart covers a wide range of topics, many of them pertaining to life's big questions. It can help illuminate our relationship to religion and what we believe in. It can reveal the areas of life in which success will come easily, and those where it may not. What gives your life purpose? How do you find prosperity and success? Do you feel 'lucky'? What does that look like for you?

JUPITER IN THE SIGNS

Aries: Jupiter in Aries makes for a natural-born leader. They have forward-thinking vision and big ideas; with their confidence and enthusiasm Jupiter-Arieans can motivate others to help them realise their goals. As long as they can be their own boss, prosperity is theirs for the taking. Those with Jupiter in this position are always working to improve themselves.

Taurus: Jupiter in Taurus is a financially auspicious pairing: Jupiter's abundance plus Taurus's predilection for financial success, means those with this position tend to have great money luck. But they also know how to put in the work. They tend to be rather conservative in their views, but have a great appreciation for material beauty, which they also have a knack for manifesting.

Gemini: When Jupiter is positioned in this adventurous, social sign, prosperity comes from travel and through the many friends and acquaintances Gemini energy attracts. Success can also be found in all fields of communication – journalism, media, academia and even theatre. Their enthusiasm runs the gamut, and they may change jobs often or even switch fields.

Cancer: Those with Jupiter positioned in Cancer tend to have luck when it comes to financial stability – opportunities come from their many connections who appreciate their cheery disposition. They hang on to money, make sound investments and find security in growing wealth. They have strong morals, a generous spirit and can find purpose in caring, parenting and creating a stable and happy home life.

Leo: Jupiter in Leo imparts a gregarious confidence – those with this planetary position are charismatic leaders, and feel especially comfortable in the spotlight, finding success in fields that draw the public eye. They are optimistic and enthusiastic, and tend to have friends in high places. They are also generous and happy to share the abundance they attract.

Virgo: When Jupiter is positioned in Virgo, the greatest sense of purpose often comes from being of service. They are practical minded and specially attuned to details – they often find success when they can put their analytical skills to good use. Abundance comes from their hardworking nature; they forge a sure and steady path directly to it.

Libra: Those with Jupiter positioned in Libra really know how to turn on the charm, and have an expansive social circle that brings them opportunities. They also find deep purpose in their desire to create and can find success in most artistic fields – their eye for beauty is innate. Libra's extremely social energy means the greatest expansion comes through partnerships and working with others.

Scorpio: When Jupiter is positioned in Scorpio, it inspires a deep and driven sense of willpower. These people also have the power of persuasion, thanks in part to their strong sense of self, which draws others to them. They are also the great secret-uncoverers, finding success in fields that require them to see past the obvious to what's hidden underneath.

Sagittarius: For those with Jupiter positioned in Sagittarius – the sign it rules – open-mindedness and optimism are the names of the game. Their growth comes through their expansive curiosity and the many experiences they are driven to encounter. Money tends to come easily, but so does their ability to spend – learning to save can be a lifelong lesson.

Capricorn: Jupiter in Capricorn often leads to great career and financial success. Those with this positioning are driven by ambition, but know the hard work and dedication it takes to get there. They put one foot in front of the other, steadily climbing their way to abundance. They find the most purpose when their means for success serves the greater good.

Aquarius: When Jupiter is in Aquarius its influence creates a progressive and innovative thinker, who will glean the most satisfaction from working in fields that will better the future. This kind of energy draws a great many friends, who often open the door to luck and opportunity. Financial abundance can be elusive, since they tend not to place a premium on material goods.

Pisces: For those with Jupiter positioned in Pisces, they will find their greatest expansion and success in the realms of spirituality and emotion. They will likely be drawn to fields that put their all-encompassing empathy to good work. Their likeable personalities draw meaningful opportunities, but they also need plenty of alone time to truly thrive.

♄

SATURN

Structure + Discipline + Responsibility

Ruling Sign: Capricorn

Transit Time: 2–3 years

After joyful Jupiter, Saturn is the cold and restrained authoritarian, here to teach us all the lessons we need to learn.

THE PLANET

Saturn is the second largest planet in our solar system – smaller only than Jupiter – and as the sixth planet from the Sun, it is nearly twice as far from that burning ball of light as Jupiter. Even at that distance it is still visible to the naked eye, and for many years was thought to represent the edge of our planetary existence, which inspired its influence over the boundaries that we set. Its rings, too, illustrate containment, and Saturn's physical distance is reflected in its emotionally removed and distant nature.

ITS MEANING

In Roman mythology, before Jupiter became god of the gods, it was his father Saturn, who ruled the heavens. In fact, Jupiter was Saturn's only child who survived, thanks to a mother who hid him from his father. When Saturn heard a prophecy that one of his children would overthrow his throne, he ate them (including Neptune and Pluto) upon their birth. All this to say that Saturn's astrological energy is one of strict authority, severity and diligent discipline. This planet is here to teach us a lesson.

WHAT IT TELLS US

Saturn's position in our birth chart influences our level of responsibility and maturity. It can help illuminate our challenges, which also helps us understand where and how we can grow. In what areas are you disciplined and what areas should you be? Where do you have structure and where do you need it? Where do you face your biggest obstacles, and perhaps more important, how do you handle them? Saturn imposes limitations and brings a dose of realism to balance out delusion. And while this all sounds like no fun at all, Saturn is truly giving us the opportunity to grow.

SATURN IN THE SIGNS

Aries: For those with Saturn in action-oriented Aries, the obstacles are many, putting a drag on their drive and repeatedly slowing their momentum. But this only serves to build great strength and courage. The older they get, the fewer obstacles they face, and with their ambitious determination, success comes much more freely.

Taurus: Saturn in Taurus can bestow a scarcity mindset. Those with this positioning may deeply desire financial security and love as well, afraid of what their life will be without them. They may pinch every penny, and stay in relationships that do not serve them, simply to abate their fear. But the determined energy of Taurus will carry them through until they do find abundance, and they tend to share it generously once they do.

Gemini: The position of Saturn in Gemini further boosts this sign's intellectual capabilities and dedication to gaining knowledge. Their difficulty may come in obtaining that education, but once they do their ability to learn, process and retain is exceptional. Saturn brings some pragmatism to Gemini's wit and curiosity.

Cancer: Saturn's position in caretaking Cancer can exacerbate this emotional sign's feelings of insecurity. They may feel the need to cling to a partner, or they may push their feelings down until they are detached and disconnected as a way to fortify their hard outer shell. Coming to terms with vulnerability and creating connections of healthy intimacy will be Saturn-Cancerians greatest challenge.

Leo: Those with Saturn positioned in Leo crave the spotlight and they can be derailed by the feeling that they aren't viewed as special. But Saturn also brings diligent energy to this regal sign, making them able to handle great depths of responsibility. Saturn cools some of Leo's great warmth, and can also hinder their ability to play, behave wildly and express themselves, especially if they don't have an audience.

Virgo: When Saturn is positioned in Virgo, its disciplined nature ups the sign's natural pragmatism. Intellectual capabilities are heightened and Virgo's attention to detail can become even more prominent. But their drive for perfectionism may likely pose a challenge, stalling their momentum, and miring them in the details and the price of furthering a greater vision.

Libra: Saturn positioned in Libra can create a fair-minded judge, someone who has an innate and impartial sense of balance. They may be known for their good impressions, as Saturn's discipline helps them control Libra's charm. Their greatest challenge may come in the realm of love, and they might experience difficulties in relationships before they learn to grow and connect with the right partner.

Scorpio: When Saturn is in Scorpio, the planet's discipline paired with this sign's watery, emotional depth and intelligence, bestows a keen understanding of the motivation and behaviours of others. This can take a turn, giving Saturn-Scorpios the ability to manipulate and dominate if they are not acting from a place of honesty. Their greatest challenge may come in the form of scandal, but they will only build themselves back up stronger than they were before.

Sagittarius: Those with Saturn in Sagittarius will probably feel as though their patience has been tried, again and again, in many different ways. This is the planet's lesson in this sign – to drive home the importance of hard work and perseverance, to help them truly earn the success that comes to them later in life.

Capricorn: When Saturn is positioned in its native sign of Capricorn it imparts ambition, determination and a fierce independence. They will likely face obstacles in their path to success, which will only underscore their desire for self-reliance. This drive to do everything for one's self, can lead to loneliness and the challenge may be to find a partner they let themself truly rely on.

Aquarius: Saturn's disciplined energy brings a wonderful pragmatism to Aquarius's grand, progressive ideas for furthering humanity. It gives this sign's proclivity for large-scale thinking a practical path for turning schemes into reality. The challenge comes from Aquarius's need for independence, which can inadvertently lead to isolation and loneliness.

Pisces: For those with Saturn in Pisces, they may find that they seek out the structure of spiritual practice. This sign's disciplined energy can turn the sign's dreamy ruminations into creative work, bringing their otherworldliness down to Earth. But they will face challenges in the realm of emotion, as they feel everything so deeply and can be quite sensitive too.

URANUS

Change + Rebellion + Revolution

Ruling Sign: Aquarius

Transit Time: 7 years

Uranus is the first of the outer planets, a cosmic surprise that is steeped in originality.

THE PLANET
For all of ancient history, Saturn held the assumed spot at the furthest reaches of our solar system. It wasn't until 1781 that British astronomer Sir William Herschel discovered the celestial body that we now call Uranus, visible to the naked eye only once a year. This first of the 'modern' planets, Uranus is seventh from the Sun and takes just over 84 years to make its full orbit. Uranus's reputation as a rebel is also represented in the way it moves through space: this planet's axis tilts so that it is nearly horizontal, so it seems to be spinning around the Sun on its side.

ITS MEANING
Although it was first named Georgium Sidus (after England's King George III), Uranus suits this surprising planet much better. In Greek mythology Uranus was the personification of heaven, the god of the sky. In astrology Uranus is the planet of originality. Its realm is the future – swift, unexpected and revolutionary. Uranus is known as the great awakener, a lightning bolt of inspiration and change. After the inner and social planets, the first of the outer planets is a cosmic visionary. Its realm is originality and how it manifests. It believes boundaries exist to be pushed. It rules innovation and speaks to a higher self.

WHAT IT TELLS US
Uranus's position in our birth chart influences our modes of originality. It can shine a spotlight on what makes us different, or amplify our eccentricities. Its placement can determine in what area of life we refuse to play by the rules – igniting our rebellious spirit and inspiring our individuality. Uranus operates like Mercury, on a higher octave, taking that planet's governing of the intellectual mind and levelling it up.

URANUS IN THE SIGNS

Aries: Those with Uranus in Aries tend to take charge when it comes to moving humanity forward. They are independent thinkers, loath to stay on the tried-and-true path, opting instead for change and innovation. Culturally speaking, when Uranus is in Aries, it can cause great and unexpected upheaval or shocking turns of events.

Taurus: When Uranus is positioned in Taurus, it lends its energy to Taurus's steady determination. The sign's need for financial security can lead to those with this placement creating innovative ways of making money or changing the way they think about resources. Culturally speaking, when Uranus is in Taurus, it can radically change our thoughts on the environment and our relationship to the planet.

Gemini: For those with Uranus in Gemini, this planet's energy is channelled into ideas. They tend to think in a different way, eschewing traditional viewpoints and relishing the freedom of progressive ideologies. They are also likely to innovate when it comes to communication. Culturally speaking, when Uranus is in Gemini it can usher in the shift of society at large.

Cancer: Uranus in Cancer can heighten the sensitivity of this watery sign. Lightning may strike in terms of their understanding of others, or deep and sudden jolts of intuition. They may find that they buck the home and family traditions in which they were raised. Culturally speaking, when Uranus is in Cancer, it can make major shifts in family life and values.

Leo: Uranus in Leo makes for expansive creativity – those with this positioning tend to have visionary artistic leanings, a deep desire to express them and the energy it takes to bring them to fruition (not to mention a taste for the public attention it can bring). Culturally speaking, when Uranus is in Leo it can bring rise to new movements, innovations or trends in art, culture and entertainment.

Virgo: For those with Uranus in Virgo, the planet's energy amplifies the sign's analytical ability, pushing the pragmatism forward with revolutionary insight. They may be highly intelligent, while thinking outside the box, putting their knowledge towards the good of humanity. Culturally speaking, when Uranus is in Virgo, breakthroughs in research or technology may be made.

Libra: Those with Uranus positioned in Libra, will often find themselves interested in non-traditional modalities of love and relationships. They may desire or create new forms of partnership. Uranus energy in Libra also makes for incredibly unique style and an often eccentric aesthetic. Culturally speaking, Uranus in Libra can inspire the sign's justice-minded ways, jumpstarting shifts in social equality.

Scorpio: Those with Uranus positioned in Scorpio tend to feel things intensely. They may think differently about their relationship to a deeper, higher level of consciousness and can pave the way for others to find that connection too. Culturally speaking, Uranus in Scorpio can lead to the transformation of society, closing one chapter to turn the page on the next.

Sagittarius: Uranus in Sagittarius bestows a need for independence and adventure and an aversion to anything overly structured or organised. People with this positioning often have a progressive philosophy about life, or explore new ways to approach life's bigger beliefs. Culturally speaking, Uranus in Sagittarius can bring new freedoms to society as a whole.

Capricorn: For those with Uranus positioned in Capricorn, they are often bestowed with the intellect and determination to change systems that no longer work. They often rebel against authority, preferring to be their own boss. Culturally speaking, when Uranus is in Capricorn, society's major systems can be reconsidered.

Aquarius: Uranus in Aquarius can lead to revolutionary thinkers. They are unique in their ability to innovate and inspire and they put their intellectual originality towards the progression of humankind. Culturally speaking, Uranus in Aquarius can spark major revolutions, and tends to be a period of great technological advancement.

Pisces: Uranus in Pisces makes for deep emotional connection, and those with this positioning have an empathy for humanity and a dreamy outlook. Their ability to innovate lies in the realm of spirituality and the arts. Culturally speaking, Uranus in Pisces can lead society to shifts in art, or new relationships to the way we view spirituality and religion.

NEPTUNE

Imagination ✦ Intuition ✦ Higher Consciousness

Ruling Sign: Pisces

Transit Time: 13–14 years

After Uranus's electric energy of change, Neptune breezes in with its mysticism.

THE PLANET
Neptune is the second of our three 'modern' planets. This celestial body was first spotted in 1791 but not officially positioned until 1846. It's the eighth and most distant planet in our solar system, residing nearly 2.8 billion miles away from the Sun. Neptune is the only planet not visible to the naked eye, which corresponds with its realm of imagination and dreams, a representation of what lies beyond the world we can see. Its cobalt hue is the result of the methane in Neptune's atmosphere absorbing the Sun's red light and reflecting the blue light – another representation of its watery energy.

ITS MEANING
Neptune is named for the Roman god of the sea, who ruled over all the world's bodies of water. Water has long represented the world of emotions, its mysterious depths a symbol of the unconscious mind and the realm of the unknown. In astrology Neptune has similar qualities. It is a transcendent planet of mysticism and spirituality. It represents our dreams, both sleeping and awake. It is a planet of illusion, dissolving the boundary of what is 'real' and what isn't. Neptune has a gentle strength, influencing our creativity, guiding our path to a higher consciousness.

WHAT IT TELLS US
Neptune's position in our birth chart influences our relationship with the realms beyond our material world. It works with great compassion, shining a light on a wide and mysterious range of ethereal realms. Are you a masterful daydreamer? In what areas does your creativity thrive? Just like Uranus and Pluto, the other celestial bodies beyond Saturn's disciplined force, it operates like one of the inner planets on a higher octave, in this case, Venus. Neptune takes Venus's love and beauty up a notch, finding beauty in all things unseen, and fuelling a deep and universal love.

NEPTUNE IN THE SIGNS

Aries: Neptune in Aries gives the active energy of this active sign an idealism that helps this generation fight for what they believe is right. They are bestowed with a fiery spirit, finding creative ways to move humanity forward. This particular pairing of optimism and determination, is fertile ground for revolution.

Taurus: For those with Neptune positioned in Taurus, they experience the expansive meeting of these two complementary energies. Deeply rooted Taurus, with its love of earthy goods, is influenced by Neptune's transcendence – a bridge between worlds. This generation understands what is truly valuable in life, rising above material trappings.

Gemini: Neptune in Gemini gives this sign's intellectual energy a deep and groundbreaking imagination. They have the mental capacity for innovation, especially in the realm of technology. Communication is key for generations with this positioning, and they will find new ways of connecting and new modes of storytelling.

Cancer: For the generation that has Neptune positioned in Cancer, they are deeply in tune with their inner, emotional lives, and driven by their sensitivity to make the world a better place. They also have a reverence for and connection to home life and family, bringing about new ways of imagining both.

Leo: Neptune's energy in this regal sign, gives those with this planet's positioning in Leo a great sense of integrity, idealism and leadership. Leo's energy brings the dreams Neptune imparts to fruition. This generation produces people who believe in a cause, rise to prominence in defence of it, and motivate others to join them with their charisma and magnetism.

Virgo: For the generation with Neptune in Virgo, the planet's high vibrations give this practical-minded sign a deep desire to be in service to humanity. But Neptune's energy can also have a befuddling effect. Virgo's clear and structured ways, can be diffused by the boundary-eliminating planet, causing confusion at a cultural level when Neptune is in Virgo.

Libra: For those with Neptune positioned in Libra, theirs is a generation driven by love – an all-encompassing love for humanity as a whole. They have a deep desire for harmony and balance and seek to change the world to bring their sense of justice to fruition. With Neptune transiting Libra, there is a societal sense of peace being sought.

Scorpio: Neptune's energy in Scorpio gives this generation the drive to uncover secrets, look beyond what they are being told and shine the light on society's darkest areas and unknown. They are bestowed with a deep connection to, and an intensity of, emotion. When Neptune is in Scorpio, society also reckons with an overt examination and exploration of taboos.

Sagittarius: For those with Neptune positioned in Sagittarius, their intellectual prowess is bolstered by idealism. Sagittarius is a sign of knowledge and learning, and Neptune's influence will help this generation bring the fields of education, philosophy and spirituality to new heights.

Capricorn: Neptune's energy in steadfast Capricorn, gives this generation the practical-minded nature to put the planet's idealism into a plan of action. Those with this positioning have the power to recreate society's structures, implementing new systems and organisations built with integrity and compassion.

Aquarius: With Neptune positioned in Aquarius, the planet brings its high vibrations to the sign's humanitarian focus. This generation is forward-thinking with great visions for a future that is inclusive, equitable and altruistically unifying. They will help usher in new egalitarian ways of existing.

Pisces: Neptune's position in the very sign that it rules, will bring a great depth of spirituality and compassion to the generation with this positioning. They will have a deep desire for human connection, for peace and transcendence. This generation may help us come to a deeper understanding of ourselves.

PLUTO

Power + Transformation + Evolution

Ruling Sign: Scorpio

Transit Time: 12–31 years

Neptune's gentle strength is followed by the intensity of Pluto, a planet that rules over power, death and rebirth.

THE PLANET
Pluto is the third of our three 'modern' planets, and its status as a planet is something that astronomers still debate. This pint-sized planet is less than half the size of Mercury, which is the smallest planet. How can that be? Although Pluto was discovered in 1930, and named the ninth planet in our solar system, in 2006 it was demoted. That's when the International Astronomical Union (IAU) redefined what a planet is, and Pluto failed to live up to its parameters. At 3.7 billion miles from the Sun, Pluto, along with its wonky orbit, takes nearly 250 years to complete one rotation around the Sun.

ITS MEANING
Pluto is named for the mythological god of the underworld, the ruler of the dead. That's appropriate for this dwarf planet at the furthest edge of our solar system, for in astrology Pluto's transformative energy rules death and rebirth. Don't judge a planet's energy by its size – Pluto is small but mighty, a planet of intensity, mystery, creation and destruction. This planet brings things to an end, so that it can start them anew. Pluto's slow and expansive orbit around the Sun, makes its transit across each sign an average of 20 years. This planet defines generations.

WHAT IT TELLS US
Although Pluto's position in our birth chart has more influence over an entire generation, this challenging, transformational, lesson-teaching planet has individual influence as well. It can preside over major life shifts. It can illuminate our deepest, darkest truths, making us face deep loss only so that we can be born again. Where and how will you find your deepest truths? Pluto is Mars in the higher octave, vibrating with its primal energy on an existential scale.

PLUTO IN THE SIGNS

Aries: Pluto in Aries ignites a trailblazing spirit – the generation with this positioning was marked by pioneering adventurousness, more than willing to leave their past behind for a promising new future. On a personal level this positioning can bestow courage, action and independence, sometimes veering into recklessness.

Taurus: When Pluto is in Taurus the planet brings its disruption to the sign's material realm. This generation fought over possessions of all kinds, and society's classes were incredibly averse and divided, the lower classes exploited. On a personal level this positioning yields perseverance.

Gemini: Pluto in Gemini transformed communication – the way information was output and consumed was forever changed. This transit also bore forth a whole generation of legendary communicators – writers, performers and, with Pluto's destructive energy, dictators too. On a personal level this positioning bestows an inventiveness.

Cancer: When Pluto moved through Cancer, the planet's transformational energy brought great upheaval to the sign's attachment to traditional home and family life. It completely restructured the way families existed, creating a paradigm shift from which new familial expectations could grow. On a personal level this positioning deepens emotions and sensitivity.

Leo: Pluto in Leo influences the rise and fall of power. This generation saw great leadership and also power gone awry. They placed a premium on celebrity, as Leo's love of the spotlight was exacerbated by Pluto. They also sought pleasure for pleasure's sake. On a personal level this positioning gives power and ego a level of outsized importance.

Virgo: Those with Pluto positioned in Virgo channel their practical natures into the service of others. This generation saw the emergence of great social movements, supporting those in need and bringing advancements in justice to the forefront. On a personal level this positioning yields enhanced analytical thinking.

Libra: Those with Pluto in Libra have a deep need for peace and a spirit bent on justice. The generation with this planetary positioning saw the end of a major war and the beginnings of peace between world powers. It saw a drive for greater equality in many realms of society. On a personal level, Pluto in Libra brings desire for harmony.

Scorpio: In Scorpio, the sign that Pluto rules, this planet's energy doubles down on the sign's realm of destruction and rebirth. The eras of Pluto's transit through Scorpio saw upheaval and revolution, violence and rebirth. The generation with this positioning is fighting taboos and clearing the way for what comes next. On a personal level, Pluto in Scorpio yields great passion.

Sagittarius: Pluto in Sagittarius makes for an adventurous generation, eager to seek knowledge and uncover the truth. This most recent era saw the rise in technological communication, democratising the media and giving power to the people. On a personal level this positioning lends a powerful optimism.

Capricorn: Pluto in Capricorn will bring the planet's disruptive energy to this sign's realm of structure and systems. The generation with this positioning will take their ambition and create new systems that better serve society. On a personal level this positioning increases responsibility and discipline.

Aquarius: With Pluto in Aquarius, this planet's energy will amplify the sign's humanitarian leanings, creating a generation bent on creating a more equitable future. The era of this positioning will likely bring about great advances in technology. On a personal level this positioning bestows a deep desire to further humankind.

Pisces: Pluto in Pisces boosts the sign's focus on all-encompassing emotions and the realm of spirituality. The era also generates a highly artistic time, producing a generation of writers, painters and more who are deeply connected to their sensitive selves. Pluto's energy will usher in a period of great love and compassion.

THE HOUSES

Understanding the energy of the zodiac signs, and the personalities of the planets, and how those personalities are affected by those energies, provides a wealth of insight into who you are and how you behave. Now we are going to add another layer of understanding to further fill in the nuances and details of who you are.

THE 12 ASTROLOGICAL HOUSES

Just as there are 12 pie-shaped slices of signs in the zodiac wheel, there are also 12 pie-shaped houses, each one representing an area of our lives. The houses run the gamut from career and finances to home and relationships. The 12 houses overlap the 12 zodiac signs in your birth chart. While the zodiac signs rotate around your birth chart, depending on your rising sign, the houses are fixed. The first house is positioned at your ascendant and goes in order anticlockwise.

THE INFLUENCE OF THE HOUSES

Understanding the houses and how they interact with the planets and signs of your birth chart, will help you understand the different areas in your life and the precedence they might take. The zodiac sign that a house is in will help you understand how that sign's energy is expressed in your life. For instance, if the third house of communication is in Aries, you probably have no problem boldly speaking your mind. If that same house is in Capricorn, you might have an incredibly practical thought process, but be more verbally reticent. Not only does the sign that each house falls in have an effect, but the placements of the planets in the different houses will determine which areas are at the forefront of your life and where the personality traits of those planets are most expressed.

WHAT'S A STELLIUM?

The placement of three or more planets in a single house (or zodiac sign) at the time of your birth is considered a stellium. Not every chart will contain a stellium, but it is worth noting if yours does. A stellium will mean that that particular area of your life will be the focus of a lot of energy, and will be heavily expressed through the zodiac sign that it is in. When it feels like that energy is throwing your life off-balance, you can address it by shifting your attention to the opposite house, or embracing the energy of the opposite zodiac sign.

FIRST HOUSE

The House of Self

Identity + Appearance + Personality

Natural Sign Ruler: Aries

Natural Planet Ruler: Mars

Opposite House: Seventh

SUMMARY

The first house is known as the house of self, and it is one of the most important houses in your chart. It is defined by your rising sign and in turn, it helps define you.

WHAT IT SYMBOLISES

The first house is a symbol of new beginnings. It marks your arrival on Earth, and the person you will be while you are here. It is a representation of who you are – your ego, your identity. It reveals how you perceive yourself and how others perceive you too. It indicates your temperament and drive, your likes and dislikes, all of the things that make you you. It is a house of firsts: first impressions and first perceptions.

It also rules our physical body and appearance. It is the packaging, so to speak, of how we present to the world. It dictates our mannerisms and personal style. It can illuminate the relationship we have to our physical selves, and the energy that makes our body feel best. The planets that appear in our first house often have a prominent influence in our lives. The first house determines where all the other houses follow – it sets the path of your astrological being.

QUESTIONS IT ANSWERS

The first house can answer a number of formative questions. How do others see you? How do you see yourself? What childhood experiences shape who you are? What are you meant to become?

SECOND HOUSE

The House of Possessions

Money **+** Resources **+** Worth

Natural Sign Ruler: Taurus

Natural Planet Ruler: Venus

Opposite House: Eighth

SUMMARY

The second house is commonly called the house of money and possessions, and its realm is that of worth – tangible goods but intangible ones too.

WHAT IT SYMBOLISES

This house rules our financial and material realm. It is affiliated with what we own, what we want to own and the kinds of things we surround ourselves with – objects, possessions and tangible assets. The second house can determine our relationship to finances – how we feel about money, what we want to use it for and how we might make more of it.

But the second house goes beyond material goods. It is also affiliated with intangible worth. It is where we hold our values, what is important and meaningful. It is also the realm of our own self-worth, and what we value about ourselves. How do our possessions fit into that and what do we place more importance on? The planets in our second house influence our relationship to money and material goods and the sign of our second house determines our attitude towards our finances.

QUESTIONS IT ANSWERS

The second house can answer a number of questions about the things we place value in. What do you own and what do you want to own? What is your relationship to money and resources? Who and what do you place value in, and why?

THIRD HOUSE

The House of Communication

Language ✦ Knowledge ✦ Environment

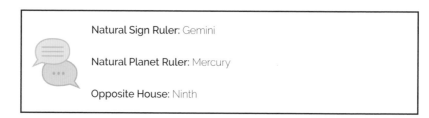

Natural Sign Ruler: Gemini

Natural Planet Ruler: Mercury

Opposite House: Ninth

SUMMARY

The third house is the house of communication – how we input, process and output information, as well as how we interact with our immediate environment.

WHAT IT SYMBOLISES

This house is affiliated with our overall style of communication and all the forms we use to relay information to others. It governs the mental processes involved with the ways in which we think, how we speak and write and the methods and language we use for both. As opposed to the first and second house, which are the realms of the self, and our material possessions, in the third house we begin to understand how we relate to those outside of ourselves.

The third house covers a number of things in our immediate environment. It not only reveals our big-picture communication, but how we interact with those in our daily lives – siblings, relatives and neighbours too. It is also the realm of daily transportation – how we get to and from where we go on a regular basis – as well as our early education and the way it set us up for future learning. Planets in our third house will relate to our communication style and relationship to knowledge.

QUESTIONS IT ANSWERS

The third house can illuminate our style of communication and everyday interactions. How best do we learn? What form of communication feels most comfortable to us? How do we share knowledge and how do others receive it?

FOURTH HOUSE

The House of Home

Family + Home Life + Ancestry

Natural Sign Ruler: Cancer

Natural Planet Ruler: The Moon

Opposite House: Tenth

SUMMARY

The fourth house is the house of home – it is affiliated with the physical environment we call home, but more importantly it relates to all of the things that make a house a home.

WHAT IT SYMBOLISES

The fourth house is one of foundation and family, of how we make a home for ourselves both literally and figuratively. Its realm covers the full circle of our lives – past, present and future too. Our relationship to our parents rests here, the nostalgia we experience for growing up, what our home felt like in childhood. It is also about our roots and heritage – the experiences of our ancestors and what we carry with us from our familial past. It is about the home we create and the one we are building for our future – what makes us feel safe, centred and whole – a dwelling, yes, but a feeling too.

This house governs the home environment but also the home within ourselves – how do we get there and what does it feel like? But it also represents what we keep in our inner sanctum, the parts of ourselves that lie in the shadows and behind closed doors.

QUESTIONS IT ANSWERS

The fourth house can reveal a lot about the foundations we build and what *home* really means. Who and what makes us feel safe and comfortable? How are we connected to our heritage and how do we put down roots? What kind of domestic space do we need to feel comfortable?

FIFTH HOUSE

The House of Pleasure

Creativity + Romance + Fun

Natural Sign Ruler: Leo

Natural Planet Ruler: The Sun

Opposite House: Eleventh

SUMMARY

The fifth house is the house of pleasure and encompasses everything that falls under this domain. If it brings us joy, it's represented here.

WHAT IT SYMBOLISES

This realm could be called the fun house. It encompasses all that brings us pleasure, from the physical plane (yes, sex is covered here) to the emotional one. The fifth house rules over all creativity – how we express ourselves, what we enjoy doing and making, the endeavours we pursue simply because they make us feel good. The themes of this house relate to what lights us up and the pure joy that makes us feel.

It is no surprise that when it comes to feeling good, sex and romance play a large part in this house. This is the realm of all-encompassing crushes and passionate flings, of brand-new romance and acts of self-love. And when it comes to sex, is there anything more primally creative than bringing forth life? Children too come under this house, along with the joy we feel in teaching and raising them. The planets in our fifth house emphasise our creative endeavours.

QUESTIONS IT ANSWERS

The fifth house is all pleasure and personal enrichment. What pastimes do we enjoy? How do we fulfil ourselves creatively? What does romance mean to us and how do we express it? Which passions spark our childlike joy? How will we create a legacy through our children?

SIXTH HOUSE

The House of Health

Wellness ✦ Service ✦ Work

Natural Sign Ruler: Virgo

Natural Planet Ruler: Mercury

Opposite House: Twelfth

SUMMARY

The sixth house, the house of health, rules the ways in which we care for ourselves and the result of that care: our ability to be of service.

WHAT IT SYMBOLISES

The sixth house is one of maintenance. It rules our health, but also all of the minutiae and daily routines that go into supporting our wellbeing, and keeping our body fit, our life humming along. Exercise, diet and daily elements of self-care are represented by this realm. So too are the roots of our worries, the things that might cause us stress and in turn, illness.

All of this maintenance goes towards keeping us in good functional health, in order that we may do our job. That's where this house's service element comes in. The work represented in the sixth house isn't career-oriented, but rather who and how we serve in our day-to-day lives, and how we feel about it on a grander scale. It governs our relationship with higher-ups and subordinates. Planets in the sixth house can reveal the nature of service that suits us, as well as the types of ways we are naturally inclined to take care of ourselves.

QUESTIONS IT ANSWERS

The sixth house covers seemingly disparate themes, but of course, they all tie together too. What type of fitness are you suited for? What constitutes wellbeing for you? In what ways do you want to be of service and how can your routines prep you for it?

SEVENTH HOUSE

The House of Partnerships

Commitments + Relationships + Adversaries

Natural Sign Ruler: Libra

Natural Planet Ruler: Venus

Opposite House: First

SUMMARY

The seventh house of partnerships rules all of our one-on-one relationships, the good (business, creative, life partners) and the bad (disputes, divorce, enemies).

WHAT IT SYMBOLISES

The seventh house represents a shift from themes of the self to themes of another, in this case partners. And not partners in the romantic sense (although marriage certainly falls under this jurisdiction), but partners more generally, anyone we have made a commitment to. This realm represents professional partnerships, creative collaborations and interpersonal relationships including long-established friendships and romantic relationships that have moved into partnerships of long-term commitment.

This house governs how we behave in these kinds of partnerships – which commitments suit us and which ones don't, what kind of partners we might try to seek. It is not only the positive, beneficial relationships the seventh house rules, but also the acrimonious ones, or the 'open enemies'. This is also the house of litigation and divorce, of partnerships broken and adversaries made. We can learn a lot about ourselves from the way we partner with others (and un-partner too), those are the lessons put forth by the seventh house.

QUESTIONS IT ANSWERS

The seventh house illuminates partnerships. What do you look for in a life partner? What do you get out of collaboration? How comfortable are you with commitment and what kind works best for you? What might lead you to dismantle a relationship?

EIGHTH HOUSE

The House of Sex and Death

Intimacy + Transformation + Mysticism

∞ **Natural Sign Ruler:** Scorpio

Natural Planet Ruler: Pluto

Opposite House: Second

SUMMARY

The eighth house is full of mystery. It rules sex, death, birth and transformation, as well as shared resources and things beneath the surface.

WHAT IT SYMBOLISES

The eighth house is steeped in mysticism (it shares that space with the fourth and twelfth houses), but is also the realm of intense life stages and such seemingly mundane things as shared assets and finances. It can be considered the house of sex, death and taxes. But what the themes of this house are truly about is transformation – death and rebirth, destruction and regeneration.

Along with sex, the most primal form of intimacy, these themes all touch on taboo. The mystery of this house is about what's lurking in the shadows, about peeking beneath the surface to become a more fully embodied human. We must experience death to know rebirth, we must endure loss to grow deeper into ourselves. The eighth house also rules over shared possessions. It governs money you may inherit, taxes filed with a partner and joint debt (some of which are results of death, so the affiliations with this house don't seem quite so arbitrary). The planets in this house will affect your own journey of birth, death and transformation.

QUESTIONS IT ANSWERS

The eighth house is shrouded in enigma, and can illuminate our dark and deeper selves. How do you deal with loss? Do you welcome transformation or resist it? What is your relationship to sex and the powerful intimacy it creates?

NINTH HOUSE

The House of Philosophy

Exploration + Knowledge + Expansion

Natural Sign Ruler: Sagittarius

Natural Planet Ruler: Jupiter

Opposite House: Third

SUMMARY

The ninth house is a house of expansion, both of the mind, through philosophy and higher education, and also geographically through travel and exploration.

WHAT IT SYMBOLISES

The ninth house symbolises growth. In its jurisdiction are the themes that help us expand our knowledge and beliefs, that rule our desire to broaden our minds and widen our world view. It is the house of higher education – how we seek, pursue and discover knowledge. It represents our major systems of belief, through philosophy, ethics and religion. The ninth house is our journey of discovery as we seek meaning beyond what we know. It is climbing up to the highest vantage point, only to look out over the expanse of land and sea and be filled with a desire to head towards the horizon.

This desire manifests geographically as well. This house is about travel and adventure. Of exposing yourself to new experiences, people and cultures. It governs long-distance journeys, and the personal growth and expansion they provide, widening our picture of the meaning the world holds. The sign of your ninth house will influence the way in which you seek knowledge, while planets in this house will signify a greater importance in your life of the themes it governs.

QUESTIONS IT ANSWERS

The ninth house reveals the way we experience growth. How do you seek knowledge? Where do you look for greater meaning in life? How adventurous are you in mind and spirit? Who or what do you turn to for spiritual exploration and depth?

TENTH HOUSE

The House of Social Status

Career ✦ Image ✦ Legacy

Natural Sign Ruler: Capricorn

Natural Planet Ruler: Saturn

Opposite House: Fourth

SUMMARY

The tenth house is the house of social status – your career, your image, your impact and your reputation. All of the things that make up your outer life.

WHAT IT SYMBOLISES

We already know that the fourth house rules our home and inner life. The tenth house is its opposite, governing our career, the work we do and the impact it has. This is the house that represents our outer life: our ambition, our drive and the recognition we receive for the accomplishments we strive for and achieve. It is about the work we are doing now, but also about whether or how that work will go on.

The tenth house is also about how we are viewed in the public eye. So yes, it is about the career path we choose and our motivation within it, but it is also about where that work puts us in the public eye. This house rules the way we are regarded by others, not only in our community but by the world. As such, it is less about who we are and more about who we seem to be to other people. We cannot control what others think of us, but this house controls who they think we are. The planets in your tenth house will have an effect on the work you do and the way it is regarded.

QUESTIONS IT ANSWERS

The tenth house illuminates much around our vocation and our status in our outer life. What work suits you best and how ambitious will your career path be? Who will your work be meaningful to? Will you reach a level of public regard for your accomplishments? And do you want to?

ELEVENTH HOUSE

The House of Friendships

Community + Social Groups + Greater Good

Natural Sign Ruler: Aquarius

Natural Planet Ruler: Uranus

Opposite House: Fifth

SUMMARY

The eleventh house governs friendships, but more than that it defines the place we find in our community, and how we work towards bettering the collective.

WHAT IT SYMBOLISES

The eleventh house governs our friendships. Not so much the intimate one-on-one connections we make, but rather our place in groups. It is our tribe, the kindred souls, the people we are drawn to and who are drawn to us. In this way it represents groups of all kinds – a group of friends, a network of acquaintances, a work-related club, a subculture or community, society as a whole. This house is about our ability to collaborate, how we relate to others and the role of teamwork in our lives.

This house also governs the role we play in bettering society as a whole. It represents ideological and humanitarian themes, like our political leanings, social justice causes and efforts we put into evolving society towards the ideals we share. It is a house of common goals and the role we play in achieving them. It is less about us as individuals and more about the harmony of humanity, moving towards a shared vision of the future.

QUESTIONS IT ANSWERS

The eleventh house can provide insight into the kind of societal collaborator we are. What role do you play in your social circles? What skills do you bring to the groups you are in? What do we do for our friends? For society as a whole?

TWELFTH HOUSE

The House of the Subconscious

Secrets + Self-undoing + Transcendence

Natural Sign Ruler: Pisces

Natural Planet Ruler: Neptune

Opposite House: Sixth

SUMMARY

The twelfth and final house is the most mystical of them all. It governs all that is unseen – secrets, dreams, shadows and healing.

WHAT IT SYMBOLISES

The twelfth house, the house of the subconscious, lies just below the horizon. It is the realm of the unseen, the darkness. It is the final house before the break of dawn, when the astrological succession begins again. The twelfth house joins the fourth and eighth house in their mysteries, but it is by far the most mystical. This house is our subconscious state, the symbolic dreams our unconscious mind produces.

The twelfth house is also the house of self-undoing. It defines our limitations, both external and internal. It governs mental illness and addiction, hospitals and prisons. It holds our karmic debt and the trauma of past lives. But perhaps the most meaningful element of this last house, is its representation of transcendence. This is where we delve into the depths and heal, reconnect with universal, unconditional love. It is the twelfth house, in all its mystery, that allows us to move forward.

QUESTIONS IT ANSWERS

The twelfth house can raise as many questions as it answers, such is the nature of this mysterious abode. But it does provide guidance. What have we buried in our subconscious that we would be better to face? Where has the life we have led brought us to? And where do we go from here?

YOUR BIRTH CHART

Your birth chart is perhaps the most important element of astrology. It forms the basis for your understanding of the celestial bodies' influence on you and your nature. But what is it and how do we understand it?

WHAT IS A BIRTH CHART?

Your birth chart is essentially a picture of the sky, the minute your consciousness came into being on Earth. It is a map that lays out exactly where the stars and the planets were at exactly the time that you were born. That's why, in order to create your birth chart, an astrologer needs not only your date of birth, but your time of birth as well. This allows them to create a chart that can pinpoint where each planet was when you began your Earthside adventure, and those placements can provide thorough and nuanced insight into your needs, wants and challenges in this lifetime.

THE TOTAL PICTURE

Although mainstream astrology focuses mainly on the location of the Sun on the day you were born, relying only on this one detail ignores the rest of the expansive sky, and provides a very broad and rudimentary take on the practice. The placement of the Sun is merely one element of what your birth chart can reveal. The sky was filled with stars and planets at the time you were born, and understanding the placement of each provides a much more detailed snapshot of what the celestial bodies can tell you.

HOW TO CALCULATE YOUR BIRTH CHART

There are many sites online that will calculate your birth chart for you, all you need to know is your date and time of birth. If you don't know your time of birth off hand, ask a parent or relative who might know. If they are unavailable or do not know, your birth certificate may include your time of birth.

THE BIG THREE

As previously mentioned, there are three signs that hold the highest places of importance when it comes to understanding your birth chart: your Sun sign, your Moon sign and your rising sign. Read on for a better understanding of what they mean and how they manifest in your life.

SUN SIGN

Your Core Personality

Just as the Sun is the centre of our solar system, it also plays the central role in our birth chart. There is a reason that this sign is the one everyone knows, even if they have only a glancing understanding of astrology. It is the best place to start when exploring yourself through the stars.

WHY IT IS IMPORTANT

The Sun is the most crucial element of our solar system, and as such it wields a lot of power in astrology. Although it is only one element of our astrological being, it is our being – illuminating the building blocks of our personality. While the other planets and placements in our chart can help add nuance and deepen our self-understanding, they are all in service of the path our Sun sign has set us on.

WHAT IT TELLS US

The Sun's placement in our birth chart is what provides the fundamental basis of our astrological reading. It speaks to who we are and how others see us. It can illuminate our behaviours, explain our motivations and help us to understand who we are at our very essence. The Sun tells us what inspires our drive; it bestows us with gifts and can help define our challenges as well. It provides a map for who we are and how we can connect with the person we are meant to be.

The energy of your Sun sign is crucial too. It illuminates the vibration that feels like home to us. It helps us understand what makes us feel best – how we experience the world and express ourselves in it too. As the influence of the other planets may come and go, the Sun is our steadfast identity from which we can learn, grow and transcend. For more information about your Sun sign, turn to the zodiac chapter that begins on page 22 and read the section for the sign that the Sun occupies on your birth chart.

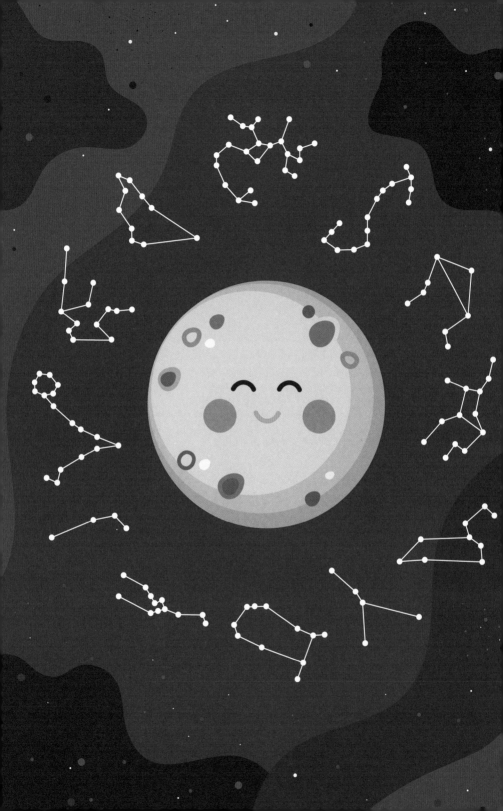

MOON SIGN

Your Inner Life

Your Sun sign may occupy the primary spot in your birth chart, influencing your personality and your outward appearance, but the Moon's position is of vital importance as well. And although popular culture places nearly all of its emphasis on the Sun sign, understanding our Moon sign helps us truly understand ourselves.

WHY IT IS IMPORTANT

The Sun represents our ego, our consciousness. It is outward action and appearance, our visible selves. But the Moon represents our instinct, our unconsciousness. It is our innermost self, our hidden thoughts and emotions, and hence can represent our truest state of being. Without the Moon's reflection to give us depth, we would have no balance, ruled entirely by the fiery ego of the Sun. It is the feminine energy to the Sun's intense masculinity. The Moon, in essence, helps complete us.

WHAT IT TELLS US

The Moon's position in our birth chart is incredibly illuminating. It shines a light on our inner core and adds nuance and depth to what our Sun sign puts forth. Its rule over the emotional realm can help us understand not only what we feel, but why and how. If our outer self feels at odds with our inner being, our Moon sign can provide the context and guidance for that conflict. It can shed light on our instinct, providing the motivation behind the things we do without even thinking about them.

The Moon's caring nature is crucial as well. It teaches us what we need to feel cared for, how we can take the best care of ourselves and how we most like to care for others. This knowledge might be the most important of all. If we do not nurture our innermost self, or offer ourselves care in the way that we need it, a true sense of fulfilment might feel forever elusive.

THE MOON IN THE SIGNS

ARIES
Honest ✦ Impulsive ✦ Idealistic

Fiery Aries leads with action, and when it comes to emotions, that can make for an intense – and turbulent – ride. Aries knows what it wants and goes after it too. You will always know where an Aries Moon stands. They are forthright with their feelings and share them honestly, even when you might not want them to. An Aries Moon feels things fast and deeply, sometimes taking a plunge without first reflecting on whether or not they should. They are ruled by passion and an optimistic enthusiasm – this dearth of processing can result in emotional risk-taking that might sometimes seem a bit emotionally immature.

Comfort & care: Aries Moons need the thrill of adventure. They love to be in pursuit of a goal and have the freedom to follow their many passions. Make them feel appreciated and you will get their best side – enthusiastic, honest and full of idealistic energy.

TAURUS
Grounded ✦ Stable ✦ Trustworthy

Taurus's fixed earth energy gives the emotional Moon a steadfast foundation from which to feel. Unlike impulsive Aries, a Taurus Moon takes their time. They ease into their emotions – slow, stable and sometimes wary too. There is no roller coaster here, just a desire for safety and a need for comfort. That want for security can sometimes lead to stagnation – they may hang on to emotions, ideas or relationships long after they have stopped serving them. They are trustworthy and loyal, a strong and faithful partner. Their grounded energy makes them physically sensitive and sensual too.

Comfort & care: Physical touch fills up the Taurus Moon cup. They are sensual beings who enjoy earthly pleasures – good food and pampering of any kind. A comfortable home makes them feel at ease and they often express themselves through the way they decorate and enjoy it.

GEMINI
Expressive + Mercurial + Versatile

Gemini is all about communication. Those with the Moon in this sign put their intellect towards their feelings. They enjoy the journey of processing emotions and are often able to merge matters of the heart with their penchant for analysis. Gemini Moons are emotionally expressive, taking you along on this journey with them. And what a journey it is! Gemini's short attention span lends itself to quickly changing emotions (the sign is ruled by Mercury, remember, from which mercurial is derived!), and their inner pendulum can swing wildly from one feeling to the next.

Comfort & care: Gemini Moons need an outlet for their near-constant expression, whether through writing, art or simply good conversation – with, perhaps more importantly, an incredibly good listener. Mental stimulation is their comfort zone.

CANCER
Sensitive + Intuitive + Protective

Cancer is the sign that is ruled by the Moon, so its placement here amplifies all those watery realms. Cancer Moons feel on the deepest level and under that hard shell they are incredibly sensitive. This extreme vulnerability can make them feel unsafe, leading to moodiness, resentment or a quick nip from their pincers. But when they feel secure and comfortable, they are incredibly attuned, not only to their own emotions, but to everyone else's as well. They have a deeply maternal spirit, a drive to nurture and a tendency to embody the role of caretaker.

Comfort & care: Trust and reassurance are what Cancer Moons need. The safer they feel, the more balanced their emotions. This homebody sign needs plenty of comfort in their domestic environment, and the space to retreat when they need a break from feeling the emotions of everyone around them.

LEO
Dramatic + Confident + Affectionate

Leo tends to be a natural-born performer, and with the Moon in this placement it is emotions that want their time in the spotlight. Leo Moons express everything with their innate flair for drama, and more than anything they want an attentive audience for their performance. Sadness, joy, love, loss – they feel it all in a big way and express it even bigger, putting it all out there for the world to see. They are incredibly warm and have no qualms about public displays of affection (in fact they relish them).

Comfort & care: Heaps of attention help make Leo Moons feel content. They like to be seen, heard, felt and understood. They love to be showered with affection as much as they love to shower others, and can benefit from creative outlets of expression.

VIRGO
Practical + Rational + Nurturing

Virgo's need for perfection can cause conflict with the Moon's watery, unorganised realm of emotions. That's why Virgo Moons can sometimes seem distant – they are applying their practical nature to something rooted in the shifting tides of instinct and intuition. Unlike big, showy Leo, they may tamp their emotions down, preferring to analyse them with their brain rather than feel them with their heart. But, with a penchant for self-improvement, they are also willing to put in the work. Virgo Moons are incredibly service-oriented. They are happy to lay low, providing nurture and support without any kind of showiness.

Comfort & care: Virgo Moons feel their best when their help is needed; this placement is at their best with a healthy outlet for their desire to be of service. They also like to know that their efforts don't go unnoticed.

LIBRA
Balanced + Accommodating + Adaptable

Libra Moons are defined by balance. They are charming, friendly, diplomatic souls who strive for a sense of emotional harmony. But this can raise issues in other areas. Their need to keep the peace can cause them to stifle their own emotions; they may lose part of themselves in their efforts to please everyone else. Because of their justice-seeking tendency to see both sides, knowing their true feelings can feel somewhat elusive. They are extremely social creatures who are masters of small talk, and they often thrive in egalitarian partnerships, romantic and otherwise.

Comfort & care: Libra Moons can be deeply romantic, so gentle gestures of love, both doled out and received, can make them feel good. These Moon signs also long for peace and feel most at home surrounded by beauty.

SCORPIO
Intense + Intuitive + Deep

Having the Moon in fixed watery Scorpio bestows an emotional intensity on these passionate souls. They are willing to plumb the depths of their feelings, however dark or shadowy they may be. And they will do the same for their friends and loved ones too, accompanying and supporting them through their own emotional journey, beyond the point when lesser-nerved Moon signs would bow out. But the intensity is a lot for these Scorpio Moons, and they can be moody and destructive, striking with their stinger when they feel slighted or wronged.

Comfort & care: Scorpio Moons value trust – it is what allows them to be open about their own emotional intensity. It is also helpful for them to have similarly fuelled emotional support around them; friends and partners who can handle their level of feelings and intimacy.

SAGITTARIUS
Optimistic ✦ Candid ✦ Lighthearted

Sagittarius has a free-wheeling nature, and with the Moon's placement here it manifests in the emotional realm. These curious, adventurous, easy-to-like people have a light hearted approach when it comes to deep emotions. They are prone to process and move on, sometimes skimming the surface of an emotional experience, and – the opposite of Scorpio – not truly exploring its deep and intense depths. They might have to work harder in order to connect on an intimate level, but as they always love to learn, they are often inspired to rise to the challenge. Sagittarius Moons are a totally honest bunch, you won't ever have to wonder where you stand.

Comfort & care: For Sagittarius Moons, freedom is of the utmost importance. Give them their space (and support when they need it) and their best qualities will come forth – enthusiasm, curiosity and a deep love of life and learning.

CAPRICORN
Controlled ✦ Serious ✦ Committed

The ambitious, pragmatic nature of this cardinal earth sign does not lend itself to the Moon's messy, emotional ways. Capricorn Moons won't give in to big feelings, they are much too controlled and reserved to let the Moon's shifting emotions get the best of them. But that doesn't mean they don't have them. This reserved Moon sign just needs a little support in order to make that inner connection, loosening the grip their logical mind has on their heart. They make incredibly dependable and responsible partners, and will put the needs and security of their family above all else.

Comfort & care: Capricorn Moons are driven to succeed and need the space and support to focus on their career. Loyalty helps them feel secure and they need that trusting environment in order to tap into their feelings.

AQUARIUS
Aloof + Logical + Forward-thinking

Aquarius is the humanitarian rebel of the zodiac, and the Moon's placement in this fixed air sign can lead them to experience their feelings at a reserve. Aquarius's rational mind does not often let itself get mired in emotions, which can make them seem somewhat detached on a personal level. But this altruistic soul always has humanity in its heart, and they are forever looking for a way to move all of us forward, however unconventional their ideas or methods might be. When Aquarius Moons do allow themselves to feel, the emotions may come fast and furious, but they will often leave just as quickly.

Comfort & care: These creative and unconventional souls need plenty of ways to nurture their non-traditional leanings. Furthering a cause and finding a community of similarly accepting eccentrics gives Aquarius Moons a place to channel and explore their world of emotions.

PISCES
Compassionate + Loving + Emotional

The Moon's placement in the mutable watery space of Pisces creates an infinite well of emotion and empathy. Pisces Moons are full of feelings and are deeply in touch with every single one. But they don't only experience their own emotions, they experience others' as well with an endlessly generous sense of compassion, and an uncanny intuition that clues them in to what others are feeling. The challenge for the Pisces Moon is learning how to control this free flow of emotional energy – setting boundaries may not come easily to them, but they can greatly benefit from establishing some parameters.

Comfort & care: These dreamy souls are also highly creative, and having artistic modes of expression can help keep them from being pulled under by their own watery depths. They also feel nurtured by time alone, especially if it involves a spiritual practice.

RISING SIGN

Your Outer Personality

Your Sun sign represents your core personality and the Moon influences your inner life, and together they paint a pretty in-depth picture of who we are. But our rising sign, or ascendant as it is also called, completes the trifecta, illuminating who we are to the outside world.

WHAT IT IS

It is clear that the placement of a planet dictates our Sun sign and Moon sign. But what is a rising sign and how is it determined? Although many other elements of your birth chart can be plotted using only your birth date, a birth time is needed for a rising sign reading. That's because it is determined by the zodiac sign that the eastern horizon line cuts through at the time of your birth. That sign changes nearly every two hours, which is why your time of birth is necessary for accuracy.

WHY IT IS IMPORTANT

Our rising sign is important for several reasons. First, it determines the placement of the first house cusp, which in turn determines the placement of the other eleven houses on the zodiac wheel. This in itself makes it an influential sign. But it is also vital as the third sign (along with our Sun sign and Moon sign) that informs our foundational astrological make-up. If our Sun sign is our core personality, and our Moon sign is our innermost self, our rising sign is our outermost self, another important element in understanding ourselves as a whole.

WHAT IT TELLS US

Our rising sign rules first impressions. It is how we look, act and appear to others we meet. It is our image, our demeanour, our outermost layers, even our physical appearance and mannerisms. Our rising sign is the airs we may put on when we are meeting someone for the first time, and the way we relate to those who do not yet know our true selves. Understanding how others see us gives us access to the full picture of how we can see ourselves.

WHAT EACH RISING SIGN MEANS

ARIES RISING
Energetic ✦ Direct ✦ Confident

Those with Aries ascendants blow into a party like a force of nature. They stand tall and impart an aura of confidence, bolstered by their energy and enthusiasm. They are lively conversationalists who don't hold back – if they have an opinion, and you can bet they do, they are going to share it. An Aries ascendant is a direct communicator, forthright about what they need and want. They tend to be impulsive too, jumping into a conversation, a project or even a job with fervour. Sometimes their fiery emotions get the best of them and they can be rash, argumentative or domineering.

Physical features: These high-energy Aries ascendants have a very physical nature too. They move through the world quickly and with agility. They tend to have strong builds and dazzling smiles.

TAURUS RISING
Stable ✦ Easy-going ✦ Sensual

Taurus ascendants have a deeply calm presence and a slow and steady nature. Their feathers are not easily ruffled, nor do they behave in any way that might ruffle someone else's. They tend to appreciate the finer things in life, and that comes through clearly in their appearance. They are put together, down to earth and prefer comfort and security over adventure or new experiences. This rising sign can appear to be stubborn if they are not careful, and resistant to any kind of change that shakes things up a bit too much. They have a sensual nature that gives them great enjoyment from life's earthly pleasures.

Physical features: Taurus ascendants tend to have an innate level of attractiveness. Their tranquil demeanour comes through in their eyes and they carry themselves with a physical grace.

GEMINI RISING
Social ◆ Chatty ◆ Curious

Those with Gemini ascendants can and will talk to anyone and everyone. They have an insatiable curiosity and are adept and charming socialisers. They feel right at home making small talk with a neighbour, mentally sparring with a colleague or dropping witticisms in casual everyday conversations. They can adapt to an environment and find ways to connect with people from all walks of life. That connection can sometimes be surface-level though – Gemini ascendants are a bit more discerning when it comes to choosing who they will truly get to know and who they will let in in return.

Physical features: The mind of a Gemini ascendant rarely takes a break, and this can lead to a nervous sort of energy, which is often dispelled by their friendly smile. They use their body to express themselves, often gesticulating as they speak.

CANCER RISING
Nurturing ◆ Gracious ◆ Reserved

Cancer ascendants are inherent nurturers and make people immediately feel cared for and at ease. They also have a deep sense of emotional intuition, which allows them to understand what someone else may be feeling and treat them accordingly. They prefer intimate connection over chitchat and small talk. Their intense sensitivity can make them feel vulnerable, so they may draw back and act reserved, but rarely forfeit their patient and gracious demeanour. But you will know when they do because the pincers come out. They have a deep sense of home and prefer to be in comfortable, familiar surroundings. Too much chaos can throw them off.

Physical features: Although their style is chic and classic, comfort rules over fashionable inconvenience. They wear their nurturing character on their face, with gentle expressions that convey their understanding and empathy.

LEO RISING
Confident + Kind + Charismatic

Leo ascendants are bestowed with an innate magnetism. They can naturally command a room and they thoroughly enjoy doing so. They feel at home in the spotlight, probably because they have the star power to sustain it. Leo ascendants seem to be steeped in confidence, and even if they aren't no one would ever know it. They are kind and charming, passionate and playful. Thankfully they're quite likeable since they like to be adored, although simply being lavished with attention is often sustaining enough. Leo ascendants also have a flair for the dramatic that they can't help but indulge.

Physical features: Leo ascendants have a commanding presence, often walking tall, with their head up and shoulders back. Their sense of showmanship comes through in their gestures and expressive face, and their style often complements their desire for attention.

VIRGO RISING
Reliable + Shy + Helpful

Those with Virgo ascendants have a polite and practical nature. Their need for perfectionism comes through in their appearance – they never look dishevelled and you won't catch them with their fly down or a button missing from their shirt. They have a deep sense of pragmatism and a keen ability to analyse. Although they are far from Leo ascendants' gregariousness, and can actually come off as somewhat shy and aloof, they have an innate helpfulness that comes through as well. Virgo ascendants are always willing to lend a hand and they emanate a reliability that others find reassuring.

Physical features: Virgo ascendants tend to be soft-spoken with a physical strength that is not immediately clear from the way they look and hold their body. Their perceptive eyes are always taking in a room.

LIBRA RISING
Social ✦ Charming ✦ Genial

Libra ascendants are in their element at a party or gathering. These extremely social creatures sweep in and sparkle, bestowing their charm and charisma on everyone in their path. They are graciously outgoing, friendly and fun – the perfect dinner guest and party-goer. They bring harmony to a room and help put everyone at ease. Libra ascendants are well-schooled in social graces – in fact they could teach the class – and have an innate sense of diplomacy. Their ability to see both sides of any story, make them fair and objective judges, but also unable to make up their mind, which can lead others to think of them as wishy-washy or unopinionated.

Physical features: Libra ascendants love of beauty translates to their appearance – they often dress well and appear to do so effortlessly (even if there was much effort involved). They also have a magnetic smile.

SCORPIO RISING
Magnetic ✦ Mysterious ✦ Intense

Scorpio ascendants may have a cool exterior, but they also have an intensity that is immediately clear. They may not share the extent of their emotional depth until they truly get to trust someone, but it is obvious there is a deepness and even a darkness churning beneath the surface. They enter a room with a powerful presence and an air of mystery – always in control and seeking to control too. They never step into the spotlight, but they command people's attention from the shadows with their enigmatic magnetism.

Physical features: A Scorpio ascendant's intensity manifests in their gaze – you may feel like their mysterious eyes can see through to your very soul. Their strength and power comes through physically as well, in the way they hold and carry themselves.

SAGITTARIUS RISING
Spontaneous + Optimistic + Outgoing

Sagittarius ascendants can be the life of the party. They have an enthusiasm for life that can be infectious, letting their insatiable curiosity carry them wherever its path may lead. Their outgoing nature makes them quick to befriend anyone and everyone and they have a sense of adventure that draws others to their orbit. Making plans is not their vibe, spontaneity feels much more comfortable to them. Those with a Sagittarius ascendant seem to embody the very idea of a 'free spirit', and a general aura of luck seems to follow them. They also tend to be incredibly optimistic, another reason others want to bask in their glow.

Physical features: Sagittarius ascendants will often have a twinkle in their eye – it hints at their enthusiasm and the adventure to come. They seem truly at home in their body and its movement, and draw people in with their bright smile.

CAPRICORN RISING
Determined + Reserved + Reliable

For those with Capricorn ascendants, it is very clear that they know how to get things done. Although they may be somewhat reserved at first, they give off a serious 'taking care of business' energy. Unlike gregarious Leo ascendants or bold Aries ascendants, they tend to hold back, assessing the situation and adjusting their behaviour accordingly. It is not until you have built up their trust that you will see this Capricorn ascendant behave wildly, which for them means cracking wise jokes or dropping their strong sense of decorum for a bit. They have a sharp intellect and an innate desire to be of service.

Physical features: Refined Capricorn ascendants tend to hold themselves with great poise. Their style tends to be simple and efficient. They carry their body in a controlled and deliberate way, assessing everyone and everything with their calculating gaze.

AQUARIUS RISING
Lively + Unique + Idealistic

It is usually easy to spot the Aquarius ascendant at a party – they will be the one wearing an eccentric outfit, chatting up everyone – no matter their walk of life – with their lively nature. Their topics of conversation will be the most unusual of the night, and they are quick to voice their very strong opinions, regardless of what others may think. They are fun, quirky and thought-provoking, with a visionary nature that comes through in myriad ways. Although they have a tendency to get along with everybody, it can be difficult to feel like you are really getting to know them as their mind is in the future, unable to meet you in the moment.

Physical features: Aquarius ascendants' liveliness comes through in their physicality – they have an ease in their body and a relaxed way of carrying themselves. They may use quirky mannerisms to express themselves.

PISCES RISING
Gentle + Sensitive + Creative

Pisces ascendants are the gentle souls who can immediately put anyone at a gathering at ease with their exceptional listening skills and genuine empathy. They are deeply compassionate, open-hearted people, and their watery ways can adjust to anyone they are engaging with. Those with a Pisces ascendant can seamlessly join in a lively and rambunctious party, or sit quietly one-on-one with anyone willing to have an intimate, bare-all conversation. They are dreamy and creative, often using a number of artistic endeavours as a means of self-expression.

Physical features: The gentle nature of Pisces ascendants translates physically as well. They tend to be soft-spoken, with an open, understanding gaze. Their body movements are soft and fluid, much like their personality traits.

PUTTING IT ALL TOGETHER

Now that you have a basic-level understanding of astrology's major themes, motifs and influences, you can use that knowledge to better understand your own astrological make-up. As we now know, you are so much more than your Sun sign! Your birth chart is full of detail and nuance, and exploring it with your newfound awareness is a wonderfully exciting adventure.

First, take a look at your distribution of planets. Are they evenly placed or do the majority fall into one of these four quadrants?

Upper Half: The outside world, sociability, extroversion and bettering the collective.
Lower Half: The inner world, privacy, introversion and bettering the self.
East (Left) Side: Independence and assertive.
West (Right) Side: Relationship-oriented and passive.

Then take a look at your 'big three' signs: Sun sign, Moon sign and rising sign. Get a feel for how the different energies resonate with you, and how, together, they embody the major elements of yourself. Look at the house that your Sun and Moon inhabit, and how their energy shows up in those areas of your life.

Next, take a look at where your planets are placed. In which house does each one reside and what does that say about you? Does one house get all the attention while others are empty? How is that energy expressed in your life? See if you can digest all this information, and distil from it certain themes, traits or energies. You might better understand where or why you face certain challenges, or what areas in life come naturally to you.

BEYOND PLANETS, SIGNS AND HOUSES

Although a lot has been covered in the pages of this book, the information truly only scratches the surface of astrology. There is so much more to your astrological make-up. Your chart is full of detail and nuance from planetary aspects (which reveals information based on the geometric relationships) to other important points, similar, although not as important, as your ascendant. You now have an illuminating foundation to work from, but, if you so desire, your astrological journey has only just begun.

USING ASTROLOGY IN YOUR LIFE

You now have the information that astrology provides, but how do you apply the magic of the cosmos to your everyday life? Astrology can be a wonderful tool for guidance, self-discovery and even self-care. Its insights into who you are, how you behave, what challenges you might face and where your strengths lie can be an invaluable input for growing into the person you want to be. Learning how the planets and their movements affect life here on Earth as they orbit the Sun can help you lean into their energy or balance it out when necessary. Above all, astrology reminds us that we are but one small part of a grand, expansive, interconnected universe, which in itself is a humbling and eye-opening experience.

ASTROLOGY AS A TOOL

Astrology is an ancient art, a reading of the stars founded on symbolism and archetypes that continues to evolve thousands of years after its creation. And astrology itself has so many layers of meaning and nuance, you can forever be finding out more and different things about the planets and their influence. On top of that, astrology is an intuitive art. Just as everyone has a birth chart unique to them, so too will their understanding and appreciation of astrology differ. In other words, there are no absolutes. Even the same birth chart can be expressed differently by different people, and every astrologer will have their own interpretation. The complexities of human existence are varied and infinite. No matter how much you resonate with the energy of your Libra Sun sign, for instance, you are so much more than an indecisive social butterfly who strives constantly for balance. If you are looking to fit your life into a neat and tidy box, with a fate determined by the stars, astrology is not it. Thankfully, too, because it is so much more!

Instead of providing a reductive definition of who we are, astrology offers us an illuminating tool that can deepen the joy and appreciation of our brief time here on Earth, raise our vibrations of self-understanding and help us to connect more deeply with ourselves and one another. Exploring your birth chart is a perfect opportunity for intentional self-reflection. It can help you take pride in your strengths and lean into your talents. You might come to a deeper understanding of your shortfalls and challenges, and an acceptance that they are an important part of who you are and your growth here on Earth. Taking the planets and the energy they express through the signs, and using the houses to understand where that manifests in your life, can empower you to work on shifting or balancing the areas where you need it most. Astrology is a framework for understanding and change. It is yours to do with as you wish, and that might be the universe's best gift of all.

INDEX

First published as *Le guide de L'Astrologie pour débutants*
in 2022 by Hachette Livre, Marabout division
58, rue Jean-Bleuzen, 92178 Vanves, France

This edition published in 2023 by Smith Street Books
Naarm (Melbourne) Australia | smithstreetbooks.com

ISBN: 978-1-9227-5424-0

Publisher: Catie Ziller
Author: Lisa Butterworth
Photographer: Lisa Linder
Stylist: Aya Nishimura
Internal design: Michelle Tilly
Editor: Kathy Steer
Cover design: Michelle Mackintosh
Project manager (for Smith Street Books): Aisling Coughlan

MIX
Paper | Supporting
responsible forestry
FSC
www.fsc.org   FSC® C008047

Printed & bound in China
by C&C Offset Printing Co., Ltd.

Book 252
10 9 8 7 6 5 4 3 2 1

NOTE: The author has researched each essential oil used in this book but is not responsible for any
adverse effects any of the oils may have. All the essential oils are used at your own risk. If in doubt,
contact a qualified aromatherapist.

ACKNOWLEDGEMENTS: It feels as if writing this book was always written in the stars, and there are
so many people who have truly helped to make it shine. Thanks to Catie Ziller for always giving me a
platform to share the things I love, Kathy Steer for her wisdom with words and Michelle Tilly for bringing
the sparkle with her designs and illustrations. Thank you to photographer Lisa Linder and prop stylist Aya
Nishimura, a visual dream team. And heaps of gratitude go to my favourite Virgo and my little Leo, I thank
my lucky stars for you every day.

CONTENTS

First published in Australia in 2023
by Thames & Hudson Australia Pty Ltd
11 Central Boulevard, Portside Business Park
Port Melbourne, Victoria 3207
ABN: 72 004 751 964

First published in the United Kingdom in 2024
By Thames & Hudson Ltd
181a High Holborn
London WC1V 7QX

First published in the United States of America in 2024
By Thames & Hudson Inc.
500 Fifth Avenue
New York, New York 10110

Universal Guide to the Night Sky © Thames & Hudson Australia 2023
Text © Lisa Harvey-Smith 2023
Illustrations © Sophie Beer 2023

26 25 24 23   5 4 3 2 1

Thames & Hudson Australia wishes to acknowledge that Aboriginal and Torres Strait Islander people are the first storytellers of this nation and the traditional custodians of the land on which we live and work. We acknowledge their continuing culture and pay respect to Elders past, present and future.

ISBN 978-1-760-76312-1
ISBN 978-1-760-76384-8 (U.S. edition)
ISBN 978-1-760-76369-5 (ebook)

A catalogue record for this book is available from the National Library of Australia

British Library Cataloguing-in-Publication Data
A catalogue record for this book is available from the British Library

Library of Congress Control Number 2023933272

Every effort has been made to trace accurate ownership of copyrighted text and visual materials used in this book. Errors or omissions will be corrected in subsequent editions, provided notification is sent to the publisher.

Design: Philip Campbell Design
Editing: Paul Smitz
Printed and bound in China by 1010 Printing International Limited

FSC® is dedicated to the promotion of responsible forest management worldwide. This book is made of material from FSC®-certified forests and other controlled sources.

Be the first to know about our new releases, exclusive content and author events by visiting
thamesandhudson.com.au
thamesandhudson.com
thamesandhudsonusa.com

For Mika Ikin, who loved our picnics on the Moon.

Universal
GUIDE
to the
NIGHT
SKY

LISA HARVEY-SMITH

ILLUSTRATIONS BY
SOPHIE BEER

Universal
GUIDE
to the
NIGHT
SKY